The Music
Business
(Explained In Plain English)

*This book is dedicated to my parents, Avner and Frankie Naggar,
to my siblings, Mickey, Auri, Ron, and Tammy,
and to my nieces and nephews,
Jed, Sari, Josh, Danny, Elizabeth and Joe.*

The Music Business

(Explained In Plain English)

WHAT EVERY ARTIST AND SONGWRITER
SHOULD KNOW
TO AVOID GETTING RIPPED OFF!

FOURTH EDITION

DAVID NAGGAR

© 2013 David Naggar
Fourth Edition. First printing.

ISBN: 978-1-57746-577-5
ISBN ebook edition: 978-1-57746-578-2

Library of Congress Control Number: 2013939969

Original cover and book design by Gary Hustwit.
Front cover image: © Nevit Dilmen
Back cover photo: © Kathy Picard

Published by DaJé Publishing, San Francisco, CA
www.dajepublishing.com
www.facebook.com/dajepublishing

Distributed by SCB Distributors
15608 South New Century Drive
Gardena, CA 90248

Printed in the USA.

TABLE OF CONTENTS

ACKNOWLEDGMENTS

No book is written in a vacuum. I have learned a great deal from all of the materials mentioned in this book. Additionally, I would like to acknowledge the assistance I've received through the years from people throughout the industry, including Jill Alofs, Fred Ansis, Chris Barros, Michael Cerchiai, Tom Chauncey, Kevin Koloff, David Conrad, Frank DuCharme, Ritch Esra, Dulce Farmer, David Gottlieb, Lyle Greenfield, Randy Grimmett, David Grossman, Edward Hearn, Susan Heller, Herbie Herbert, David Hirshland, Jim Kennedy, Jeff Leslie, Jeff Lowy, Harry Poloner, George Scarlett, David Shea, Ron Sobel, Bruce Solar, and Don Welty. I'd also like to thank Kathy Picard for her assistance in reviewing this book. Finally, a special thank you to Jeffrey Brandstetter. Without his work on the first edition, this book would not exist.

FOREWORD TO THE FOURTH EDITION

Much has changed in the music industry since I wrote the third edition of the Music Business (Explained In Plain English). Sales of physical CDs have continued to decline, and digital distribution methods have evolved. Major label record companies are regrouping to take full advantage of the emerging digital, streaming, cloud age. Music markets and audiences are even more fragmented. New sources of income for artists and songwriters are replacing older sources of income, and many artists are more hesitant than ever to sign *any* record deal, as record companies seek to sign artists to deals in which the record companies profit not only from record sales, but also from other sources of artist income such as live performance, publishing and merchandising.

Even though there are important new players in the industry, the dominance of major label record companies continues — at least in terms of breaking out new artists and overall digital and CD sales. Beyond new methods of music distribution, new business models for streaming music, new copyright rulings and regulations, new rules for licensing songs, and the emerging use of cloud lockers, there is a growing importance for artists to build their own websites and fan base.

This updated and expanded edition covers these changes, and more. As with the first three editions of this book, I've made every effort to explain what artists and songwriters need to know in plain English.

INTRODUCTION

1. THE BOTTOM LINE

Music is art. This book is not about art!

There is a harsh reality about the music business that you probably already know: **People (not counting loved ones) will help you if they think your art will make them money. They will not help you if they do not think your art will make them money.**

Like other businesses, the multi-billion dollar music industry is driven by money. Because sales of physical CDs have tumbled, large record companies are not in the best of financial health. This too is a harsh reality of the music business. But the music business itself is not going way. It is merely morphing.

If you are new to the music business, or have been involved for years but never really had "the big picture" explained to you in plain English, this book is for you. I have written it to help artists and songwriters understand the basics of this industry beyond the club scene, and beyond the process of creating your own fan page or uploading your music for direct purchase. You don't need to know everything, but if you don't understand the basics, you are setting yourself up to be ripped off.

I've used a lot of footnotes because I am a lawyer and lawyers do that sort of thing. The information contained in the footnotes is important to clarify nuances, but is less important than the main text for understanding the big picture. Also, I have tried to be specific about real numbers used in the industry, such as the royalty percentages earned by artists signed to record deals and the royalty rate earned by songwriters when their songs are put on those records. Although I know these numbers are important to you, keep in mind that the numbers can change very quickly, and many times, during the course of your career. The concepts, however, remain the same and are the heart of the big picture.

Let's get started...

2. SOURCES OF MUSIC INDUSTRY PROFITS

There are many sources of profit for musicians — and everyone else in the music business. Money is made from the sale of physical CDs, digital downloads, interactive streaming, getting songs played on the radio, on television and in films, from concerts, video games, ringtones, merchandising, advertising, endorsement deals, and more.

Many performing artists can make a little money by nurturing a small fan base, creating a website, and establishing an account with an online music distributor.

However, today, for almost all performing artists, the real money flows first from making a record deal. This is because good record companies excel at promoting and building an artist's brand so that the artist can reach out beyond a small fan following. Establishing a great brand (and avoiding getting ripped off along the way) leads an artist to be in a position to financially benefit from multiple income sources in the music business.

It may seem old-school that the *catch* for an artist to participate in the music bonanza is getting a good record deal in the first place. You may have read multiple articles that highlight declining CD sales and the struggles of record companies. Yes, sales of recorded music have slowed, but sales still bring in $10 billion to $20 billion dollars annually around the globe. Arctic Monkeys — the band that many people hail as one of the first internet driven success stories — did not cash in on the music bonanza until after signing a good record deal. And Justin Bieber — who was discovered by a talent manager who saw Bieber's videos on YouTube — didn't start generating serious money until his hookup with Usher and Island Records.

Here is the hard part. **As an artist**, until you create a *buzz* in the industry, it is extremely unlikely that you will get a good record deal. Absent a buzz, industry pros won't think they can make money from your art — and no one will spend the resources on you to see that you have a big money-making music career.

Of course, in today's Twitter, Facebook, YouTube, MySpace, Google, iTunes world, once you become a famous artist, you may no longer need a record company for future financial success. But to help you become famous in the first place, a record company's participation may be indispensable.

You may be both an *artist* and a *songwriter*. Yet to follow the money flow, never confuse the terms *artist* and *songwriter*.

As a songwriter, you make money from the act of having written a song, whether you perform the song yourself, or other people perform the song. If you are a songwriter, your real money flows mostly from getting your songs on what the industry calls *records*. *Records* means CDs, digital downloads, vinyl, and all other formats. If the artist (or artist's decision making representative) doesn't think that putting your song on a record will ultimately bring the artist more money than not having your song on the record, then your song won't be on the record. Don't count on any exceptions to this.

Remembering the distinction between *artist* and

songwriter **is the most important key to understanding how you will make a living outside the club scene in the music business.** When I use the term *artist*, I am talking about the person who performs the song, whether live or on a record, regardless of whether or not the artist wrote the song. When I use the term *songwriter*, I am talking about the person who wrote the song, whether or not the songwriter performs it. Adele as an *artist* and Adele as a *songwriter* makes money in different ways for the performance of her songs (as an artist) and the writing of those same songs (as a songwriter).

Now, let's talk about the artist side of things...

BASICS FOR THE ARTIST

3. THE ARTIST'S BUSINESS ADVISORS

If you are an artist, there are three important advisors who will help you make key music business and career decisions: your personal manager, your attorney, and your agent. There are good personal managers, attorneys and agents out there, but there seem to be many who are not. Do not deal with anyone you do not instinctively trust.

The more high-powered, respected advisors you have on board, the more likely you are to get a record deal from a reputable record company.

SPECIFICS ABOUT YOUR PERSONAL MANAGER

The personal manager is the most important member of the three because if you get a good one, a record company is going to feel comfortable that there is someone keeping an eye on your music business life for you. Executives at the record company are then more likely to think that you will generate income for them — i.e., record sales and other income.

A good personal manager will advise you regarding all aspects of your career. Personal managers are responsible for promoting you, advising you about what songs to record, who to hire as your producer, who to sign a recording contract with, and when and where to tour. They also coordinate publicity campaigns and insulate you from time demands such as interview requests. The hands-on personal involvement each personal manager actually provides varies greatly.

The vast majority of personal managers receive between 15% and 20% of the artist's *gross* earnings as compensation. The percentage is negotiable, and depends not only on the extent of service that will be provided, but on the experience of the manager as well. In my view, it is worth hiring the best personal manager available, without regard to the exact percentage being paid. It is a better career move to part with 20% of gross earnings in order to hire a talented personal manager — one who can actively promote you and knows many people in the industry — rather than insisting on paying only 15% for someone who cannot further your career. When you become highly successful and the total dollars you earn grow wildly, you can then negotiate to lower the percentage a personal manager receives.

When negotiating with a manager, try to exclude from the definition of *gross* earnings — earnings on which the manager gets paid — items that are not truly income, but rather are what I call "pass-throughs." Two examples of pass-throughs are 1) recording funds that the record company gave you, but that you used to pay the studio or other musicians, and 2) money given to you by the record company to help cover the cost of touring that, in turn, you used to pay other people on the tour. Your manager should not be paid on monies that come to your account, but that you don't actually keep.

The term of a personal manager's contract is typically three to five years, but the term may be tied to album release dates or tour schedules rather than to actual fixed calendar dates.

Make sure your contract with a personal manager states that he or she will be the person primarily representing you, rather than someone to whom the manager delegates responsibilities. Your contract should also include a provision allowing you to cancel the contract if, for example, you are not earning a certain amount by a given date, or have not received a record deal by a given date. Otherwise, you may be stuck for a long time with a personal manager who is taking you nowhere.

You should also be certain the contract clearly states the amount of money your personal manager is to receive from earnings on deals you made *during* the term of the contract, but occurring *after* the expiration of the term. As an example, if you sign a deal to record five albums with Interscope Records, and soon thereafter you have a falling out with your manager, should the manager receive 20% of all future profits? Clearly, that would not be fair, especially since your new manager will want 15% to 20% of your entire gross income whether or not you are still obligated to pay the former manager. Limit the percentage amount and length of time after the termination of the contract that a former manager receives payment.

Here are some other critical questions you want to ask before you hire a manager:

1. Does he or she *really* like your music? Managing your music career is hard work. If you don't sense that your music is loved, the manager will inevitably work less hard.

2. Who does he or she know in the music industry? The more relationships you can verify, the better.

3. How many other artists does he or she manage? In

other words, how much time will the manager really have to devote to you and your career?

Surprisingly, some of the industry's top managers do not have written contracts with their artists — just a handshake — and the only discussion point before hiring the manager is the percentage of your income the manager receives. All is left to good faith! While this may be a reality, it is *not* a good practice. As long as the relationship is going well, a handshake may be fine. But the moment things turn sour, you and your manager are likely to have very different ideas of what "the deal" was.

SPECIFICS ABOUT YOUR ATTORNEY

Attorneys specialize in different fields of the practice of law. A great corporate attorney may know absolutely nothing about the music business. It is important to hire an attorney who is knowledgeable specifically about the music business because attorneys in the music business are heavily involved in negotiating and structuring the deals artists make. There are so many hidden pitfalls buried in music industry contracts, hiring an attorney who understands the interplay between language and numbers is critical. One artist's 14% royalty on record sales may make the artist rich, while another artist's 14% royalty may pay that artist nothing.

As an artist, you must make sure you understand *in advance* how your attorney is going to charge you. Often, music attorneys use a retainer as a minimum payment against which they charge a flat hourly rate or "value" billing amount.[1] Expect to pay $300 an hour and up for a good music attorney in Los Angeles and New York, and a little less in Nashville, San Francisco, Miami, Atlanta and other major markets. Some music attorneys, if they strongly believe the artist will be signed to a record deal, or the artist is already established, will forego a set fee in exchange for a percentage of the artist's earnings that flow from agreements the attorney negotiates on the artist's behalf (typically 5%). More and more, the most powerful attorneys in the industry insist on using this latter billing method. Obviously, it is to their advantage, not yours.

Here are some critical questions you want to ask before you hire an attorney:

1. Does he or she specialize in music law? If the answer is no, this may not be the right attorney for you, no matter how much you like the attorney personally.

2. Who does he or she know in the music industry? Again, as with the personal manager, the more relationships you can verify, the better. If the attorney has access and is trusted, your record or publishing deal will move more quickly.

3. Who else does he or she represent? If the attorney has seen a lot of deals, he or she will know how much a record company will part with to make your deal. There is one matter, however, to be careful about. In the music industry, attorneys, or the firm at which an attorney works, often represent both record companies and artists. You don't want your attorney to negotiate a less favorable deal for you so that he can continue to do other legal work for the record company. The conflict of interest is real, and so are the lawsuits that stem from this conflict.

---

1 With "value" billing, an attorney charges you based on his or her estimation of the value of the services rendered to you. Generally, a billing practice in which attorneys assign a value to their own work is not a great system for you, but it is what it is.

SPECIFICS ABOUT YOUR AGENT

Music agents book concerts and other personal appearances. But music agents are not as powerful as their counterparts in the film and television business. In some cases, particularly in country music, agents are completely bypassed. In any event, I suggest you allow your personal manager to help guide your decision of which agent to pick because it is your personal manager who will be dealing with the agent most of the time.

Many agents agree to be bound by entertainment union contracts: AFM (American Federation of Musicians) contracts for musicians working as instrumentalists; and generally, AFTRA (American Federation of Television and Radio Artists) contracts for vocalists.[2]

These unions each have their own printed form contracts that agents and agencies use.[3] With few exceptions, these unions allow agents to charge only 10% of an artist's gross earnings in the areas in which the agent renders services. Therefore, agents do not get a portion of the artist's income from records sales, songwriting or publishing. (AFM and AFTRA's printed forms actually do have a place for the artist to initial that gives agents earnings from records; *never* agree to this.) Some music agents are anxious for business and discount the percentage of the artist's gross income they receive to well below 10%. If an artist

---

[2] Agents agree to be bound by other entertainment union contracts, as well: AEA (Actors' Equity Association) for stage performances, and SAG (Screen Actors Guild) for a vocalist's performance captured on film.

[3] If you sign with a major agency, they will have you sign agreements from all of the unions.

is generating major income from concerts, the fee from concert income may be as little as 4% to 5% (or even less if the agent really wants a big name act on his or her roster).

Generally, agents will want you to sign a contract that lasts for three years, but in some cases no contract is ever signed. As an artist, try to limit the term of the contract to one year if you have the negotiating strength. This will allow you to move on if your agent is not performing well. It will also allow you to renegotiate a lower fee if you are generating major dollars.

There are many important terms to negotiate before signing with an agent. Your attorney and personal manager can help you with these. For instance, the scope of the agency must be understood. Is your agent in charge of lining up *all* concerts and personal appearances, or something less? Also, the geographic territory in which the agent represents you, and the specific duties of the agent in obtaining and negotiating the terms of your engagements, must be agreed upon. Even more esoteric items, such as which union form governs when union forms overlap or contradict each other, must be negotiated. Make sure your attorney reviews the terms of your agency agreement. Otherwise, it could cost you a lot of money!

♪ ♪ ♪

In addition to these three key advisors, when you actually have money coming in from a record or publishing deal, you will also need a business manager/accountant who is deeply familiar with the nuances of the music business. The business manager/accountant will make sure your tax situation is straight, will review royalty statements, assist in managing the financing of your tours, offer investment advice, and manage your money.

Since your attorney and personal manager will almost certainly be in place before you need a business manager, they will be able to guide you in picking a business manager.

4. SENDING OUT YOUR MATERIAL

Many artists make the mistake of sending a demo CD to everyone they know *before* creating any local interest in their music and *before* having any of their business advisors in place. This is not an effective way of getting discovered. At a cost in excess of $1 to make, package and send your demo, you would be better off playing the lottery.

Rather than sending demo CDs, some artists simply send unsolicited mp3 files to record companies. Others opt to send links to their website or Facebook page. Doing either is not an effective strategy for getting signed.

Until you have music business advisors in place, your demo cannot be shopped to the powers at a major record company in earnest. First, create a buzz about your music — have a database chock-full of devoted fans — *then* have a business advisor shop your demo. The buzz is what will bring record industry people to hear you.

As an artist, material you send directly to an established record company will generally not be listened to, no matter how good it is. In part, this is because record companies fear potential liability in accepting material they have not asked for (what the industry calls *unsolicited* material). They do not want to be the target of a lawsuit by a disappointed artist who later claims that his or her song was stolen and used by the record company.

Additionally, you should know that record companies receive more demos than their key personnel have the time to listen to. Therefore, the ones that actually do receive fair consideration are almost always received from professional managers or music attorneys who are known to the key people at the record company. These demos are also of high quality (sonic quality, not necessarily good music).

As the industry matures and morphs to use different business models, most major label record companies are looking to sign artists who have already established record sales histories. They sign artists who have released their own CD to the public or have had their music repeatedly downloaded — artists who have demonstrated an ability to generate sales without big label promotion. So, build your web presence, let record companies see that you have a loyal fan base, and show them you are serious about your career. Like all businesses, record companies are looking to lower their risk. This risk averse attitude has been heightened in the wake of economic fears and personnel cutbacks caused by internet piracy and lower sales.

Despite the advice I've offered above, if you choose to send out your own material directly to record companies, then at the very least, make sure that the material is "solicited,"[4] and send it to a particular named person in the Artists & Repertoire department of a record company (not "Attention: A & R director at Sony"). Send a CD with three to six songs on it. Make sure your contact information is on the CD itself. Save the expense of sending lyric sheets and your press clippings,[5] but if

---

[4] It is better to telephone in advance — even those people who will accept unsolicited material — to ask if you can send them your music. Making it solicited gives your material a greater chance of being heard in the best light possible. Call to confirm that your demo CD has arrived, and follow up with a call a couple of weeks later to confirm that the CD has been listened to. Remember though, if you do send out your own material, it is extremely unlikely to get serious consideration.

[5] There are still many CDs received by A & R departments. Most lyric sheets and "puff" material will likely be separated from your CD well before it is listened to. If someone at the A & R department likes what they hear, you'll be asked for more.

you think your photographic image is a strong selling point (e.g., you are a drop dead hunk, drop dead gorgeous, or so bizarre you absolutely must be noticed) include it as well. Today, image can be as important as talent in convincing a record company to partner with you.

The only time that you, as an artist, will send your material to a publishing company is if you are also a songwriter. Publishing companies make money from owning rights to songs, not from signing artists. A major publishing company will not offer you (the *songwriter*) a publishing deal unless they are fairly certain they can get you (the *artist*) a record deal, or unless they love your songs and you agree to have others record your songs. Once you've read this book, you will understand the economics of why that is. So, for an artist who is also a songwriter, the publishing deal often comes as a part of the record deal itself, or after the record deal is made.

If you want to be an artist, I recommend that you *not* sign a publishing deal until you are signed to a record deal, or until you are convinced you will not be signed to a record deal without a publisher's help (i.e., if you have been rejected by the record companies you want to deal with, or can't even get your foot in the door).

A good place to find a list of names, addresses and key people in the A & R departments of most every established record company is in the A & R Registry published by The Music Registry, www.musicregistry.com (but this PDF download costs money). You may also have luck finding A & R people in the All Access Music Group database, www.allaccess. com. Access to this database is free.

5. RECORD COMPANIES & DISTRIBUTION

In record contracts throughout the industry, a ***record*** is considered *any* device that can transmit sound, and also *any* transmission method that delivers music. This broad definition includes physical CDs, DVDs, vinyl records, videos, and delivery of music via the internet or via any other electronic method. An ***album*** has traditionally been defined as 8-12 selections (songs), with approximately 45 minutes of playing time.

The record business is evolving from a business driven by physical record sales, to one driven by digital delivery of music. Yet physical CD sales still exceed digital album sales. The complete destruction of physical sales has not occurred as rapidly as some expected. Older music fans haven't fully embraced digital delivery. They rarely download music. And, digital downloads as a delivery method — both singles and albums — may suffer in the future as streaming and cloud sharing models change the landscape.

The massive internet disruption aside, the record business has always been cyclical. It does well in good economic times, and poorly in bad times. In good economic times, record companies fight over artists and make deals that are better for the artists. As I write, we are not in good times.

RECORD COMPANIES

If an artist signs a recording contract with a record company, the artist will go into a studio and record songs for the record company. The record company then makes copies of the master recording (or subcontracts the making of copies to a manufacturing company) and ships these records to a *distributor*. The distributor is the wholesaler who sells the records to the retail stores (like f.y.e.). The record company also handles and controls the artist's digital distribution — what record companies call *electronic transmissions*. With distribution in place, the record company gears up its advertising, promotions, sales, etc., and voila, everyone is working together toward the artist's stardom.

I tend to categorize record companies into four groups: major label record companies, major label affiliate labels, independent labels (whose records are distributed through a major label) and true independent labels.

MAJOR LABEL RECORD COMPANIES

The biggest record companies are called *major label* record companies. Many of these companies, such as Arista, Atlantic, Capitol, Columbia, and Virgin are identified in the pages that follow. Take a look at your collection of CDs. The better known artists are usually represented by major labels, and the major label's name will appear prominently. When you download music, the label's name will also be there.

Many divisions of a major label record company are important to an artist's success. Although your record deal will be negotiated with the Business Affairs Department (home of the lawyers), the most important departments for your success are the A & R Department, the Marketing/Sales/New Media Department(s) and the Promotions Department.[6] **If you and your personal manager are friends with the key people in these departments, you are much more likely to be successful. As**

---

[6] Not every major label record company has the same identical departments; nor do they identify the departments that serve particular functions by the same name as other major label record companies.

the legendary Joni Mitchell says, it's "stoking the star-maker machinery behind the popular song."

1) The A & R Department

People in the A & R ("Artists & Repertoire") department act as the "ears" of the record company. They are the folks charged with finding new artists and working creatively with them. However, just because an A & R person loves your music and helps you sign a deal with the record company does not mean that you are destined for stardom. Your record still has to be released, and it still has to sell. The path to glory is littered with artists who were already preparing themselves for stardom to strike after recording an album, only to discover that the record company decided not to release their album!

Understand that most of the people in the A & R department of a major record company are not as important, in terms of deciding which artists get signed, as some would have you believe. Most of these people are under the age of 30 and are hired because they have convinced someone higher up in the company that they can spot and deliver talented artists to the record company.[7]

The reality is that the dollar commitment a major label makes when it signs a new artist can be several hundred thousands of dollars in recording costs, pressing and distribution, promotions, marketing, tour support, etc. A chief executive, such as the industry famous Clive Davis, may hire someone to screen talented artists from the non-talented ones, but *he* and a few key advisors will be making most of the final decisions.

---

[7] In the past few years, A & R staffs were cut. For instance, a few years ago, Columbia Records had 17 A & R people at its New York headquarters. Today, few remain.

2) The Marketing/Sales/New Media Department(s)

These people are in charge of getting traditional retail and online stores excited about carrying your record. They oversee album-cover artwork, promotional merchandise, advertising for your album, web page creation, in-store displays, and publicity.

3) The Promotions Department

The people in the promotions department are in charge of getting artists' records played on traditional and online radio. They do a lot of traveling to schmooze key radio station personnel so that your record gets played. If it doesn't get played, how is anyone going to know to buy it? The not-so-funny joke in the industry is, "How can you tell if a record is going to be a hit? Look at the promo budget."

♪ ♪ ♪

As I will discuss in the next subsection, major labels are either owned by, or are financially linked to, conglomerates which own the large distributors. These large distributors, in concert with major labels, have more sway with record stores — online and brick — than independently owned distributors.

MAJOR LABEL AFFILIATE LABELS

Major labels often have special relationships with smaller labels whereby the major label may fund the smaller label's recording and operating costs in exchange for part of the smaller label's profits. The line between a major label affiliate label and an independent label whose records are not funded by a major label, but are distributed through the major, is often blurred.

INDEPENDENT LABELS
(Whose Records Are Distributed Through A Major Label)

These record companies have few, if any, full-time employees. An independent label signs artists and sees to it that the records are recorded. Often, the independent label contracts with a major label to perform the promotion, marketing and many other paper-intensive functions of a record company. Many major label distributed independents earn their keep simply by finding talented artists and making sure that the major label record company actively markets and promotes those artists.

TRUE INDEPENDENT LABELS

A true independent label has no association with a major label. Unlike major labels, major label affiliate labels and independent labels whose records are distributed through the major label network, truly independent labels distribute their records through *independent distributors* not associated with the majors.

♪ ♪ ♪

Which record company you choose to sign with is critical to your career. Do not go with the biggest just because it is the biggest. Your art may not get the full attention it needs to help you succeed. If people in the marketing department are busy pushing Beyoncé, they may not have time for you. Meet with key record company personnel who will be charged with marketing and promoting your record before signing a deal. With an independent label, this may only be one or two people. Ask how they usually go about marketing and promoting an album. How committed are the key people to your album? Do they like your music? Will they push it even if it isn't initially successful? How much time and money are going to be spent marketing and promoting your album?

Remember, you will not be signed unless the people at the record company believe that your music will make them money. It does help if key record company personnel actually like your music because if they do not, you will be dropped more quickly from the company roster should you not be making money for the company right away.

Major label record companies are signing fewer new artists and shrinking their rosters as they cope with difficult financial times and less revenue from music sales. Keep in mind that the short-term profit motive is strong at major labels and their affiliates. Even if you are signed, and key personnel do like your music, you are likely to be dropped from the label's roster if you aren't a success soon out of the box. And, if you are dropped, a stigma attaches, and it will be difficult for you to get signed to another major label, ever. Many artists are eager for a shot, and sadly, it still seems that major labels will churn talent in the hopes of finding an instant star, rather than developing one. If the industry *buzz* and sales track record you created — i.e., the work that got you signed to a major label in the first place — does not translate quickly into profits, the label will replace you on its roster with a new artist who has industry buzz. If the industry operated thirty something years ago as it does now, Bruce Springsteen, whose first two albums weren't commercially successful, would have been dropped and probably never heard from again.

Finally, when deciding which label to first sign with, keep in mind that each record company is unique. Each has its own strengths in different styles of music. Since the music industry is notoriously known for its personnel changes, the best way to know what services are offered by a particular record company is to ask (e.g., how they handle distribution, what resources are available to market and promote records, what previous success they've had getting radio play for artists who play your style of music, what plans they have for exploiting digital delivery systems).

THE DISTRIBUTION SYSTEM
(OF PHYSICAL RECORDS)

How consumers buy (or pirate) music has dramatically changed in the past decade. The traditional record store of 10 years ago failed due to increased competition from mass merchant stores such as Wal-Mart and Best Buy, legal internet downloads and subscription streaming services, and a massive amount of music piracy.[8] Over 1,000 specialty music stores closed in the last decade, including all of Tower Records' stores and Virgin Megastores. On a national level, only f.y.e. remains — though not really as a music only specialty store. In the last few years, mass merchants have dramatically reduced the amount of floor space devoted to music. Today, iTunes is by far the largest music retailer on the planet.

For the most part, neither smaller music stores nor mass merchants will carry an artist's record unless the record has a distributor. With the exception of internet sales of *physical* records, a strong distribution system is critical to ensuring that enough of your records are going to be found in enough places to sell enough copies to make money for everyone involved in the process of making and selling a physical record.

---

[8] The power shift in the music business continues to play itself out. A few years ago the Eagles distributed their album, *Long Road Out of Eden*, exclusively through Wal-Mart. AC/DC, Miley Cyrus, Kiss and Journey struck similar deals. It wouldn't make financial sense for these artists to do so today.

Keep in mind that a fairly large retail record store — if you are lucky enough to still have one in your town — can physically only carry 60,000 to 70,000 total CDs, but there are many more CD titles than this in print. Even if the store carried just one copy of every CD title, not every CD could be in the store. And in reality, a huge store will have many copies of the most popular CDs, and few, if any, of lesser known CDs. As for the smaller brick and mortar stores that sell music, only the most popular titles will be carried.

These facts lead to one of the biggest advantages of signing with a fully staffed major label, if you can. Major labels' records are distributed by large distributors, and large distributors are better able to get stores to stock the labels' records for two reasons: 1) they have more people available to do the work, and 2) these records will be more widely promoted and marketed. These two reasons explain why major labels are also best positioned to do a better job at digital distribution through the internet. After years of consolidation, there are only three major national wholesale distributors left in the U.S., and all three are connected on a corporate level to many major label record companies. They account for roughly 80% of all U.S. record sales:

> **Sony Music** (distributes Arista, Columbia
>   Epic, RCA, Capitol and Virgin)[9])
> **Universal Music Group** (distributes Interscope,
>   Island/Def Jam, and Motown)
> **Warner Music Group** (distributes Atlantic, Elektra
>   and Warner Bros.)

---

[9] Each of these major distributors distributes records for many other record companies as well. For instance, see Warner Music Group's complete record label roster at www.wmg.com.

Even though so-called independent distributors — such as Caroline Distribution — have become wholly owned by Sony, Universal, or Warner, there are still a variety of smaller national and regional independent distributors who are truly independent. Because contracts between distributors and retail stores generally allow the retailers to return copies of records that do not sell, a distributor's cash flow can be erratic. All of the records a distributor thought it had sold to f.y.e might come back to it a few months later. This is why some smaller independent distributors are constantly on the brink of financial failure. Others are not particularly reputable. For example, a decade ago, Tower Records had a vendor list of about 250 independent distributors. While some of the distributors merged operations, the vast majority simply went out of business. Before going bankrupt itself, Tower had culled its vendor list down to 80 vendors.

If you are considering selling your own *physical* CD through an independent distributor, make sure the distributor is in sound financial condition. Here's an oversimplified example of why — it involves looking at two contracts: first, the one between you and the distributor, and second, the contract between the distributor and the retailer. Suppose you "sell" your records to the distributor on January 15. Your contract with the distributor is likely to state that the distributor must pay you sometime in April. In the meantime, the distributor "sells" your records to f.y.e., for example. The distributor's contract with f.y.e. will state that f.y.e. must pay for your records sometime before the end of March (i.e., before the April date the distributor agreed to pay you). So far, so good.

But remember that in the music industry, most contracts between a retailer and a distributor allow the retailer the right to return to the distributor any record the distributor previously "sold" to the retailer that the public didn't buy.[10] If f.y.e. decided in March to return to your distributor two thousand records of other artists that f.y.e. could not sell to the public, but for which f.y.e. already paid the distributor in December of last year, then the distributor owes a refund to f.y.e. on those two thousand records. Even if f.y.e. actually sold all one thousand of *your* records to the public, since two thousand is more than one thousand, your distributor actually owes money to f.y.e., not the other way around. By April, the distributor will also owe you money for your one thousand records sold. You have been out of pocket the cost of making the CDs since January 15, but, by the end of April, you may find that the distributor has paid its own salaries and overhead but has no money left over to pay you. The moral is: check the distributor's financial statement before signing the contract!

Although it is usually better to have a major distributor distributing your records, depending on the style of your music or where you expect your record to sell, this may not always be the case (assuming the independent is financially sound).

Independent distributors have less leverage to get brick and mortar record stores to carry a particular CD, and frankly, sometimes independent distributors serve as a weigh station for smaller labels and artists who are on their way up (or on their way down). Nevertheless, independent distributors, such as City Hall, may serve your art better than a major distributor.

---

[10] Most distributors actually do charge retailers a penalty for returning too many records, but in all practicality, the problem of more returns than sales remains. Note also that tight inventory controls at retailers means that a new record may stay in the store for only 90 days, if not less, before it will be returned to the distributor as unsold.

For example, independent distributors are significant players in distributing newer styles of underground music. Also, because they are typically less bureaucratic, independent distributors can place product into their system and solicit orders more quickly than a major label record/distribution company can.

A traditional distribution entity — major distributors and independent distributors — buys from manufacturers (i.e., record companies) and sells directly to retail stores. These distributors also sell records to sub-distributors known as "One Stops" and "Rack Jobbers" who have niche markets:

ONE STOPS

One Stops carry records from many record companies; hence, *one stop* shopping for the retailers who wish to purchase these records. One Stops sell records used in jukeboxes, and also sell to mom and pop retailers in small quantities. The markup to mom and pop retailers is generally higher than it is to stores such as f.y.e. or Best Buy.

RACK JOBBERS

Rack Jobbers buy records from traditional distributors, and then resell them to merchants. Wal-Mart, which sells a high percentage of all physical CDs sold, uses a rack jobber. In essence, rack jobbers operate as a store within a store, overseeing merchandising, marketing, and even product returns.

♪ ♪ ♪

Record companies also license others to manufacture and sell the record company's records to consumers, thereby bypassing the traditional distributor. Examples of such licensees are: 1) foreign distributors of U.S. records; and 2) television packagers who sell CDs through TV ads (e.g., a "special" Frank Sinatra CD marketed on TV that is advertised as unavailable in any store).

DISTRIBUTION THROUGH THE INTERNET

Digital distribution eliminates many inefficiencies in the industry, including the cost of manufacturing copies of CDs that may not sell, the cost of shipping CDs across the country, and the business transaction cost associated with the record stores having the right to return unsold product to record companies. Since the whole point of distribution is to get records to places where the customer can make a purchase, the internet is a magnificent tool for record label distribution.

The internet allows record labels and artists to distribute records directly to music fans. Record labels are still feverishly fighting to limit and control digital piracy by filing lawsuits, and sponsoring legislation. Yet for the most part, digitally encoding songs to prevent copying is a thing of the past.[11]

"Free" peer-to-peer sites, such as Grokster, were forced to close, having lost a landmark Supreme Court case in 2005. Napster, once infamous for music piracy, is now legitimate, owned by streaming service provider Rhapsody. And the legality of cloud sharing music files between friends is yet to be completely sorted out. Still, what is clearly pirated is massive.

---

[11] Digital encoding to prevent the copying of music is legal, and is commonly referred to as digital rights management (DRM). The practice has now been abandoned by all the major labels.

Free music seems to be only a mouse click (or YouTube) away.

Yet paying for music is also only one mouse click away. The dominant forms today are downloads and streaming. Streaming services like Spotify and Rhapsody still lose money, but Apple, Google and Amazon are eager to find ways to make this music delivery system work profitably.

Many people view the internet as the great equalizer that takes power away from the major labels and their distribution dominance. Though many factors have contributed to shrinking profit margins in the industry, major label records still account for the vast majority of digital sales — about 85%.[12]

Still, with the advent of online distribution companies such as CDBaby, any artist can bypass a record label and place his or her record in a virtual store such as Amazon.com or on an mp3 site, and their fans can then purchase a hard copy, download the music or just stream. Digital distribution may not succeed in actually placing your CDs in physical record stores, but it gains you access to the ever increasing digital world.

And since iTunes accounts for over 60% of all digital downloads, just having access to this one delivery mechanism potentially puts your music in front of a tremendously wide audience.

INDEPENDENT DIGITAL DISTRIBUTORS

Three of the better known digital distributors are CDBaby, TuneCore and MondoTunes.

---

[12] This according to Nielson Soundscan.

CDBaby — CDBaby charges a one time set up fee per album, currently $49. CDBaby will pay you 91% of the money it receives from download sites such as iTunes, and subscription sites such as Spotify and Rhapsody. See www.cdbaby.com.

TuneCore — With TuneCore, you will receive 100% of the money it receives from sites such as iTunes or Spotify, but TuneCore charges $29.99 per album for the first year, and $49.99 each year thereafter. If you want to distribute a single song, the fee is $9.99. See www.tunecore.com for more details.

MondoTunes — MondoTunes charges a one-time fee of $37.99 per album, $24.99 per EP (three to six songs), and $7.99 per single to distribute music online. It pays 100% of the money received for digital downloads. It also offers other services to help with marketing. See www.mondotunes.com.

CDBaby and MondoTunes are also able to provide physical distribution of CDs. If you are starting out, I recommend MondoTunes or CDBaby. If you are certain that you are going to sell one thousand downloads every year, using TuneCore may be worthwhile.

Also, if you go this route, consider services from ReverbNation (www.reverbnation.com), Orchard (theorchard. com), Nimbit (www.nimbit.com) and Amazon's Createspace (www.createspace.com).

Unlike a deal you may enter with a major label, with these particular digital distributors you don't sign away long-term exclusive rights to your music. So, the big financial downside of "Oh, my God, what did I do!" is not present. Still, be very careful regarding the contracts you enter into on the internet. Make sure you understand what you are agreeing to. Digital-land is not free from unscrupulous characters.

♪ ♪ ♪

The challenge for the unknown artist, from a business point of view, is to alert enough people that the artist actually has a product worth purchasing. You can offer to sell your songs at a site like iTunes or allow streaming at Spotify or Rhapsody, but the internet hasn't disrupted the dominance of the majors yet. The web is full of clutter, and you still need to differentiate yourself from everyone else who places music on the web.

The truth is, most artists who do their own promotion sell few records. Few artists ever make even $1,000 selling their music on the internet.[13] Without the muscle of record labels to arrange media publicity, promote radio and web play, and obtain prominent placement in traditional and online record stores, a major independent internet sales breakthrough from an unknown artist will likely be the exception, not the rule.

More likely, if a little known independent artist's internet sales or streaming numbers show promise, a major label will step in and offer the artist the major promotion dollars necessary to take the record, and the artist's career, to the next level. It is then in the artist's court to decide whether the artistic possibilities and trade-offs of signing a deal with the major label are worth it.

Whether or not the internet is an equalizer of sorts, if

---

[13] One exception is Bishop Allen. The band's members haven't struck it rich, but they've made money, are still playing music, garnishing publicity, and plugging away.

your aim is to have a record that will generate huge sales and huge profits — to have a hit record — you are much more likely to succeed if you sign a deal with a major label record company.

♪ ♪ ♪

Let's discuss how an artist profits from CD sales, digital downloads and streaming.

6. ARTIST ROYALTY RATES & PAYMENT CALCULATIONS

The most sought after contract in the entire music industry is a record contract. For making a record, an artist gets paid a portion of the money the record company takes in from record sales. This artist's portion, which is an amount negotiated between the record company and the artist, is known as the artist's royalty.

Having a basic understanding of the way in which royalty payments are calculated is critical to your understanding of the amount of money an artist can make from a record. In negotiating a record deal, an attorney who is familiar with the nuances of the music business and has a good sense of numbers really helps. Take to heart what I said earlier. One artist's 14% royalty may make him or her rich, whereas another artist's 14% royalty may yield the artist nothing.

A record store may sell a CD for a *suggested retail list price* ("SRLP") of $17.98 or $18.99. Most will discount this price. The mass merchant stores will often sell CDs for deeper discounts. No matter the SRLP or the actual price paid by a fan, the royalty rates in most record contracts being signed today are calculated on the basis of what is called the *published price to dealer* ("PPD"), not the SRLP. (I'll talk about royalties from downloaded music and from streaming later in this Chapter and in Chapter 7).

Today, the PPD price on most top-line CDs is between $9.00 and $10.00. This is the wholesale price charged to music retailers. For the most part, retailers that sell more CDs are in a better position to negotiate a lower wholesale price.

Here are some typical artist royalty rates. The actual royalty rate, of course, will depend on the artist's negotiating strength. *These royalty rates are the **base rates**, and in many record contracts the rates are lowered if certain criteria are not met:*[14]

For a new artist who has never had a record deal, or a signed artist who has never sold more than say 100,000 albums of any record, a typical royalty rate will be 13% to 16% of the PPD if he or she is signed to a major label record company. The range is a bit wider if signed to an independent label.[15]

An established artist whose last album sold 200,000 to 400,000 copies is likely to be able to negotiate a royalty rate of 15% to 17% of the PPD.

A major star whose last album sold 750,000 copies or more is likely to command a royalty rate of 18% or more.

Expect royalty rates for downloaded singles and albums to be the same as the royalty rate for the sale of physical CDs.

Royalties paid for physical singles sales are normally three-quarters of the royalty rate paid for CD album sales, but record companies rarely release physical singles.

---

[14] Generally, the major labels apply the base royalty rate only to records sold at 1)at full wholesale price; 2)in the U.S.; 3)on their main label (many majors own subsidiary labels, and this can affect royalty payments); 4)through retail record stores; *and* 5) through a record company's normal distribution channels. Royalty rates for the same record are different depending on the method of distribution! Various types of reduced royalty rates are discussed in Chapter 7, "Other Artist Royalty Rates."

[15] A few labels still base royalty rates on a percentage of the SRLP (or use 130% of the actual wholesale price, not the PPD, to calculate royalties). These formulas are more complicated and involve more deductions than the newer "simpler" formula of royalty payment calculation based on the wholesale PPD.

As you can see, the more sales the record company expects to generate from an artist's record, the higher the percentage they will be willing to pay the artist. Also, an escalated percentage of the PPD on each individual album can be negotiated. For instance, the artist may receive only 13% on the sale of the first 100,000 units, 15% on the sale of the next 200,000 units and 17% on sales of units in excess of 300,000.

Now that you know the general royalty rate percentages various artists receive, you also need to know that artists don't actually receive their full royalty rate in payment. By way of example, an artist with a CD royalty rate of 17% of the PPD will not actually pocket 17% of $10.00 ($1.70) for each CD sold. An artist's royalties from a gold album (i.e., one selling 500,000 copies) will definitely not generate $850,000 ($500,000 x $1.70) in artist's royalties. Not even close.

There are many deductions from the $850,000 found in every record company contract. But, the types of deductions, and the amount of those deductions, are different in each record company's form contract. And contracts do change. In all of these contracts, the deductions must be reviewed carefully. Let's look at some of the typical ones.

A REAL WORLD EXAMPLE OF A ROYALTY PAYMENT CALCULATION

(This stuff is a little dense. Alright, maybe more than a little dense, but it's important that you have an understanding of how this works.)

If, for example, an artist's royalty *base rate* is 15%, the artist's royalty would be $1.50 per CD (15% x $10.00 — I'm using $10.00 but the actual PPD may be less).

Most often, the artist's royalty rates are called ***all-in***, which means that the artist is responsible for paying his or her record producer out of the artist's share of royalties. Typically, the record producer receives a royalty of 3% to 4% of the PPD.[16] Therefore, if the artist has to pay the producer from the artist's share, the artist's remaining share may only be 12% of $10.00 ($1.20) — e.g., the artist's all-in share of 15% less 3% paid to the producer.

Also, royalties are paid only on records "sold." "Sold" is defined in an unusual way in the record business. Often, it turns out to be only 90% of records actually sold,[17] so the artist in our example actually receives only $1.20 on 90 of every 100 CDs sold. The artist gets no money on 10 of every 100 CDs sold!

Assume 200,000 CDs are shipped to stores:	200,000
Times: Royalty per CD that goes to the artist	x $1.20
Times: Royalty-bearing percentage	x 90%
Gross Royalty to the artist	$216,000.00

When calculating the amount of royalties to actually pay the artist, the record company withholds a part of what it may owe the artist. (That's right, you don't get the $216,000 yet.)

---

[16] In music genres such as rap or hip-hop, the person mixing the songs may also get a small royalty that is considered a part of the artist's *all-in* royalty payment.

[17] This is because most record companies give retailers "free goods," or otherwise discount the total price of CDs to entice retailers to stock more physical CDs. This is one way to push the sales of CDs, but doing so lowers the royalty paid to the artist. While record companies may call their "free goods" by another name, they still only consider 90% of records they really sell to retailers be counted as "sold." Thankfully, it is unnecessary for record companies to give "free goods" to digital distributors.

The record company withholds part of what it may owe to the artist because contracts between distributors and record stores generally allow records sold by the distributor to the store to be returned to the distributor if the public isn't buying the record. Distributors receive the same type of return privilege from record companies.

This is important to you as the artist because *all* of your records can be returned if the public isn't buying them! The record companies and distributors argue that they do not know which records will come back to them even though computer tracking makes this less true today than ever before.

The money the record company holds back and does not pay the artist because of this return privilege is called a ***reserve***.[18] Reserves may be held for as long as two years before they are finally paid to the artist.

Typically, a record company withholds paying an artist 20% to 40% of the royalties that would otherwise be due to an artist if the record store's purchase of the artist's CD from the record company were final and not returnable. The exact percentage the record company withholds from paying the artist is negotiable and depends on the artist's previous sales track record as well as sales expectations for the artist's next album.

For rock artists and newer artists, a reserve of 30% to 40% is more common because a seemingly hot rock star's album may go cold in a hurry, and the record sales a new artist can generate are unknown.

---

[18] There is no reserve on downloads, since downloads can't come back.

Continuing with the example of royalty payments from the previous pages:

Gross Royalty (from the previous pages) $216,000.00
Less: 30% reserve (typical of a moderately
   successful rock artist)   − $ 64,800.00
                                     $151,200.00

As an artist, you may never see any of the $216,000, let alone the $151,200, because of *advances* and *recoupment* of advances.

Here's how advances and recoupment work: A record company often pays out money to the artist, or on the artist's behalf, before records are sold and royalties are earned. This is called an *advance*. For instance, the cost of going into the studio and recording the record is treated by the record company as an advance payment of record royalties to you.

An advance is not only the money paid directly to the artist or paid on the artist's behalf to the studio where the record is made. Also treated as an advance is money paid to the producer and to studio musicians hired for your project. In addition, typically 50% of the cost of "independent" promoters (i.e., people hired by the record company who aren't employees of the record company but are nevertheless hired to schmooze with radio station personnel so that your record receives radio play), and 50% of the cost of making a promotional video are considered to be advances. And, if the record company helps pay for part of the cost of your tour, most likely all of this cost will be considered an advance against your record royalties. In some record contracts, the items considered *advanced* are painstakingly listed and can be a page long.

Typical recording fund dollars advanced by a record company are listed below. What isn't actually spent on recording — studio time, musicians, producers, etc. — is kept by the artist:

New artist signed to an independent record company — $0 to $100,000
New artist signed to a major label record company — $100,000 to $250,000
A moderately successful artist — $300,000 to $750,000
Major star — $1,000,000 or more[19]

Independent promotion, inexpensive videos and tour support can easily run another $150,000 to $200,000. When money is made from selling a record, the record company keeps all of the artist's royalties to pay itself back before the artist gets paid anything. This is the *recoupment*. The record company is recouping what it advanced the artist, and this may mean that the artist never actually receives any royalties from the record company, unless the artist's record is very successful.

In our example of 200,000 CDs shipped to record stores, if the record company advances $150,000 to cover the costs of recording, and advances another $150,000 to cover the cost of some independent promotion, or to help underwrite the cost of a tour, the artist owes the record company $148,800 ($300,000 less the $151,200 royalty earned), assuming the 30% reserve of the records "sold" to the record stores go unsold to the public and are eventually returned to the record company.

---

[19] Often, when the artist has signed a record contract to record multiple albums, the advance to the artist for making any album other than the first one is stated as a percentage of the royalties earned from the artist's previous album. However, there is usually a minimum and a maximum that the record company will be obligated to advance irrespective of the actual sales of the previous album. The minimum protects the artist from a small advance if the previous album was a bomb, and the maximum protects the record company from paying a huge advance if the artist's previous album sells millions and millions of copies.

Not everything the record company pays for, however, is an advance. If the artist has negotiated his or her contract well, the following are not typically charged to the artist's account as an advance by the record company: manufacturing and shipping costs of a record, marketing/sales department(s) expenses, and promotions department expenses.

In addition, there are a few other deductions from the amount actually paid to the artist. While all deductions should be reviewed with your attorney before you sign any contract with a record company, the biggest ones are that no royalty payments are made on either 1) real free goods, or 2) promotional copies of records.

As discussed, free goods are records given by a record company to retailers as an incentive to get them to carry more of a particular record the record company is trying to push.

Promotional copies are given free by record companies to radio stations and others in the industry who help promote records. They are not supposed to be for sale, but unfortunately, promotional copies often end up being sold.

If the royalty earned by the artist doesn't cover the amount of the advance (this actually happens a lot), the artist is said to be "in the red" and has a deficit. This amount is typically carried over to the next record through what is called *cross-collateralization*, which means that the artist won't see any of his or her royalties earned as an artist from the next record (even if it is a hit) until the deficit from the first record is paid back to the record company in full. If there isn't a second record, the record company generally swallows the loss and the artist is no longer responsible for it.

If you are an artist and a songwriter, never allow the royalty payments due you as an artist from your record deal to be cross-collateralized with royalty payments due you as a songwriter for having written the songs on the album. (Royalties earned as a songwriter will be discussed in the next part of this book, which is about songwriter basics.)

So how much of a royalty does an artist make on a rare gold album? (Remember, a gold album is one that sells 500,000 copies.):

CD (published price to dealer — PPD)	$	10.00
Times: Net royalty rate to artist		
(15% "all-in" less 3% to producer)	x	12%
Gross Royalty per CD (12% of $10.00)	$	1.20
Times: 500,000 albums	x	500,000
SUBTOTAL		$600,000.00
Times: Royalty-bearing percentage	x	90%
Gross Royalty		$540,000.00
Less: Typical recording costs and other		
promo/video/touring/advances		
(some paid to the artist)[20]	−	$300,000.00
TOTAL ROYALTY TO THE ARTIST		$240,000.00

This amount is probably not as much as you thought a gold record would earn. And because reserves are typically 20% to 40%, the artist will get only a fraction of the $240,000 until perhaps two years later. Further, the amount of the total deductions may be much higher. The point is, even a gold album

---

[20] Recording funds advanced to an artist to cover recording costs that are not spent are kept by the artist. But don't count on much money being left over unless you are a major star with a major budget.

could easily leave an artist in the red, owing money to the record company. A high royalty rate may be something people like to brag about at cocktail parties, but stated royalty rates are only part of the equation and can be misleading. If you are reviewing proposals from several record companies, compare the bottom line dollars going into your pocket. Do not be fooled into focusing on the royalty rate itself.[21] Ask for a description and real life examples of how the royalty rate translates into actual dollars. Doing this will help avoid confusion and disputes later on.

ROYALTY PAYMENT CALCULATION FOR DOWNLOADED MUSIC

Royalty calculations for downloaded music are pretty straightforward. There are no free goods and there are no physical returns to complicate matters. The price paid by Apple and other online music sellers to record companies for downloaded albums is 70% of the selling price. At a price of $9.99, this amounts to roughly $7.00. If the artist's royalty rate is 15% "all-in," the calculation would be:

Assume 50,000 albums are downloaded
  from online stores such as iTunes: 50,000
Times: Artist's net royalty percentage
  (e.g., $7.00 x 12% — remember, 3% of the
  15% goes to the producer)   x $0.84
Gross Royalty to the artist $42,000.00

---

[21] Royalty rates are often structured in ways that are much more complicated than the example above, but the principles are the same. For instance, many royalty rates are based on the sales of the previous album or on the average sales of previous albums. Also, the stated royalty rate for any given album may increase when certain levels of sales are achieved. For instance, the royalty rate might be 13% of the PPD for the first 100,000 albums sold, 14% of the PPD for the next 100,000 albums sold, 15% of the PPD for the next 100,000 albums sold, and so on.

If you bypassed a record company and use a distributor such as CDBaby to distribute your album, you would keep all the money paid to CDBaby by the music seller on your behalf, less CDBaby's cut of 9% of the download price.

For downloaded singles, the artist's royalty is a percentage of what the record company receives from the download music seller. For each track downloaded from iTunes at $0.99, major labels receive about $0.70 from Apple. The price paid by Apple to the record company varies if the download price of the track is more or less than $0.99. Digital distributors such as CDBaby seem to receive a couple pennies less per track from Apple. According to CDBaby, after CDBaby takes its cut, the artist typically receives about $0.60 on a $0.99 cent download.

For artists signed to a label,
the following royalty calculation is based on
downloads of 200,000 singles from iTunes: 200,000
Times: Artist's net royalty percentage
(e.g., $0.70 x 12% — remember, 3% of the
15% goes to the producer)   x $0.084
Gross Royalty to the artist $16,800.00

The small payment to artists stemming from downloading singles is the reason many big name artists are reluctant to have their music sold this way.

And, as with royalties on physical CD sales, the artist may not actually receive these royalties if the artist owes the record label money for production costs, advances, cost of touring charged to the artist, previous album losses, and so on. This is not an issue if the artist uses his or her own distributor for downloaded music sales.

ROYALTIES FROM CABLE TV, SIRIUS XM AND STREAMING SERVICES

Royalties from cable TV music channels, satellite radio operator Sirius XM, and music streaming websites such as Spotify, Rhapsody, iTunes Radio, Pandora and Google Play Music All Access also put money into record company coffers.

There are many different digital music delivery models, some of which include a video stream. The amount and method of payment *to record companies* (the typical owners of the rights to the recording) varies by service type. For instance, payment can be a percentage of ad revenues or a fee per record track streamed. Record deals typically call for the artist to receive the full royalty rate on all income that a record company receives from digital streaming. If an artist has a *base rate* 15% royalty rate, the artist gets $15 for every $100 the record company takes in (less applicable deductions). But there are exceptions that come into play for songs played on cable TV music channels, satellite radio and **non-interactive webcasts** if the service providers opt to operate under a governmental *statutory license* rather than under a contractual license with the record company. (Non-interactive webcasts are webcasts that don't allow listeners to pick their own songs to listen to — like Pandora's). When statutory licenses are used, artists are paid directly by a non-profit organization called SoundExchange, rather than by the record company. Sirius XM and Pandora both currently use statutory licenses. But to put streaming into economic perspective, one million streams on Pandora will only net the artist a little over $500.

That artists receive such a small amount of money for the streaming of their music has caused an uproar in the music community, yet music streaming services counter that they pay out millions of dollars and are not yet profitable.

Some in the industry place blame for the small payments to artists squarely on the record companies rather than on the digital streaming companies. They believe the small payments artists ultimately receive from digital streaming through the record companies is unfair because record companies pay artists more for other record company licenses, for example licenses to play parts of an artist's record in a movie or on a television show. If history is a guide, as more dollars are generated from digital streaming, artists' attorneys will be in a better position to negotiate a higher percentage of streaming income to flow to artists. (I discuss streaming in more detail in Chapter 7, and movie and TV licenses in Chapters 22 and 23).

♪ ♪ ♪

One final important point about the money an artist actually gets to keep: the record producer's royalties are calculated somewhat differently. Remember, the producer's royalties are paid out of the artist's share of royalties.

Traditionally, producer contracts state that the producer is not entitled to payment of his or her share of the PPD until the artist's recording costs have been recouped by the record company. However, once the artist's recording costs have been recouped, the producer's royalties are owed immediately and must be actually paid to the producer for every record then sold.

In other words, if a record company was fully recouped when the sales of an album reached 200,000, the artist would finally actually receive money (the artist's percentage of the PPD) on the next album sold. But when that album is sold, the producer is entitled to receive his or her share of the PPD on all 200,001 albums sold! Because of this anomaly, and because the artist may still be in the red from a previous record (due to cross-collateralization), or other advances, the artist can be responsible for paying the producer a lot of money even though the record company doesn't owe the artist a penny. **Therefore, it is generally a good idea to insist that the record company be responsible for paying producer royalties in the event of a shortfall.**[22]

And so you know, advances paid to producers are all over the map. The advance depends on how sought after the producer is, and the budget of the project. New producers can make up to $30,000 to produce an album, but often, there are several producers on an album, each producing a few songs. Somewhat established producers can make up to $50,000 per album. Sought-after producers working on an album with a larger budget expect a much larger advance, as much as $25,000 per song.[23]

Many major label record companies are now directly advancing to the producer a portion of the recording costs that used to be advanced to the artist. This is especially true if the producer has his or her own studio. Even in this scenario, the money advanced by the record company to the producer is still subject to *recoupment* from the artist's royalties before the artist

---

[22] Of course, the record company will extract other concessions for agreeing to do this, and will add the money it pays the producer to the amount *advanced* to the artist. Other than as noted above, and in this footnote, producer royalties are generally calculated in the same way as artist royalties. The exception to this is for audio-visual sales. In that instance, the producer gets half of the customary royalty (on the theory that the audio — as opposed to the video — portion of the master is only half of the product).

[23] In addition, sometimes a separate "mixing fee" is paid to the person who performs the final mix-down, blending the many tracks of a recording project down to two-track stereo. A great mixer can receive over $10,000 per song.

sees a penny from record sales.

As for your deal with your producer(s), the producer is getting paid to produce, often quite handsomely. If he or she expects a publishing interest in your song because of some minor contribution made in the process of production, this can cause friction and lead to disputes down the road — especially if the song is a hit. Make sure you've discussed your expectations with the producer in advance, and do your utmost to contractually keep your producer away from your publishing income. Of course, if you really are co-writing songs with your producer, the producer deserves songwriter credit and publishing income participation.

7. OTHER ARTIST ROYALTY RATES

An artist's royalty rate on the same record varies depending on the method of distribution and sale, and on the type of license the record company (or government) grants to those who wish to use the record as part of a business or project. Below are important royalties (and royalty rates) that an artist may receive. Actual payment to the artist of these royalties is subject to the same deductions discussed in Chapter 6.

1) MID-LINE RECORDS

After the new record has had its initial run and is no longer being actively promoted by the record company, it becomes what is called a *catalog item*. Typically, catalog items are sold to retailers at a reduced PPD (65% to 80% of top-line new release records — thus, mid-line). A record that is a catalog item, or is otherwise sold by the record company to retailers at a reduced 65% to 80% price, carries a reduced royalty payment (typically 66.67% to 75% of the artist's base royalty rate discussed in Chapter 6).

2) BUDGET RECORDS

These records are sold to retailers at an even more reduced PPD. You see them selling at the store for less than 60% of the price of top-line new release records. The artist's royalty rate on budget records is typically 50% of the base rate.

3) CUTOUTS AND DELETES

Cutouts and deletes are records removed from the record company catalog because the record is *really* dead. Artists get no royalties if these records are sold. They are being sold at a loss. If you've thumbed through CDs in the junk bin of a record store hoping to find a great buy, you've found the cutouts and deletes.

4) GREATEST HITS ALBUM

An artist's royalties for a "Greatest Hits" album are based on a blended rate of the royalty rates the artist received from the albums on which each song first appeared.

5) COUPLING AND COMPILATIONS

Coupling occurs when two or more artists appear on the same album. When many artists appear on the same album, the album is sometimes called a compilation album. The total royalties generated by such albums are split among the artists.

6) DUETS, TRIOS AND MORE

When two artists record the songs on an album together, royalties from the album are split 50%/50%. If three artists are recording together, the royalties are split equally as well. Sometimes two artists agree to perform a single song on the other's upcoming album. In this case, generally, neither artist (nor record company) pays the other.

7) MASTER USE LICENSE (INCLUDING FILM SOUNDTRACK ALBUMS)

Fees, rather than a royalty, are usually received by record companies for licensing the use of their artist's master recording in film, television, advertisement and video games. Record companies typically pay the artist 50% of the *net* money received for granting the license. What record companies are allowed to deduct from the *gross* money received, to arrive at a *net* amount to split with the artist, is worth fighting over. Typically the artist's 50% *net* is really only 37.5% to 42.5% of the money.

8) FOREIGN ROYALTIES

These vary widely depending on the artist's recognition in a particular country. In Canada, the royalty rate is typically 85% to 90% of the base rate. In industrialized nations such as the United Kingdom, France, Italy, Germany, Japan and Australia, the royalty rate is typically 70% to 85% of the base rate. In what is referred to in a typical record contract as "Rest of World," the royalty rate is typically 50% to 66.67% of the base rate.

9) PUBLIC PERFORMANCE OF A MASTER

In many foreign countries, TV and radio stations pay money to the record company for playing a record (i.e., playing "the master"). TV and radio stations in the U.S. *do not* currently make such payments to the record company. There is no legal obligation to do so. There are, however, rare *voluntary* exceptions. For instance, because Clear Channel Communications wanted to stream Fleetwood Mac's new four-song EP on its online music service, iHeart Radio, it agreed to pay Fleetwood Mac — which owns and controls its own master of the new EP — a sliver of its am/fm radio advertising revenue when songs from the EP are played. Big Machine Label Group (home of Taylor Swift) cut a similar deal.

But record companies are pushing Congress to enact the Performance Right Act. If ever enacted, this will require U.S.-based TV and radio stations to pay record companies for playing their records. Make sure your contract requires your record company to pay you for the public performance of your record if the record company gets paid. The only time the record company shouldn't have to pay an artist when the record company is paid is when the artist is entitled to be paid directly for the public performance from a performance rights society such as SoundExchange. (When payment from SoundExchange comes into play is discussed on page 46 and in subheading 10 below, about digital performance royalties).

Note also that U.S.-based record companies have typically refused to pay the artist royalties for foreign performances of a record because the record companies claim the artist can apply directly to a foreign rights society and collect his or her share. Unfortunately, most U.S.-based artists aren't eligible to collect these monies. With the growth of the international market, requiring payment from the record companies for these performances is increasingly worth fighting for.

10) DIGITAL PERFORMANCE ROYALTIES (AND STREAMING)

Electronic transmissions of music include any method of delivery that doesn't come with a physical product like a CD or a vinyl record. The Digital Performance Right in Sound Recordings Act of 1995, and the Digital Millennium Copyright Act of 1998, set the stage for your record company and you, the artist, to have the right in certain cases to receive royalties when the record is digitally transmitted.

For the artist, what's most important to know is this: Sirius XM satellite radio and internet radio webcasters, such as Pandora, must pay to broadcast a public performance of a record, even though U.S. am/fm radio stations have never had to pay.

In the case of cable TV music channels, satellite radio, such as Sirius XM, and **non-interactive webcasting** — where the user doesn't select what song to listen to — the broadcasters may elect to pay a statutory license fee to a non-profit performance rights organization called SoundExchange rather than negotiating a fee directly with the record company. The amount paid to SoundExchange depends on the webcaster's size and service rendered, and is either a fraction of a penny per audio stream, or a percentage of the webcaster's gross revenue. SoundExchange distributes the fees to the record company and the artist directly. If SoundExchange is involved, after deducting its own administrative fee, the money collected is split 50% to the record company, 45% to the artist, and 5% to a fund operated by musician unions.

In the case of **interactive audio streaming** on demand, such as Spotify and Google Play Music All Access — where the users can choose what song to listen to — only the copyright owner of your master recording, typically the record company, has the right to charge the streaming service a fee. This fee is either a percentage of advertising revenue and/or an amount per each subscriber to the service. If the record company is the copyright owner of your master recording, you, the artist gets your royalty from the record company. The payment calculation is derived from your base royalty rate. If your rate is 15%, and the record company received $100, you get $15 (less deductions).

Today, digital streaming is growing in popularity, and artist revenue from digital streaming will likely grow over time — assuming, that is, that streaming becomes more profitable. But even as more music lovers grow content with having access to music, rather than feeling the need to own the music, digital streaming services remain unprofitable (though the financial markets value these companies as if they will be profitable in the future). Just as an artist earns very little from Pandora, a streamed play on Spotify earns the artist very little. Spotify pays the record company 0.5 to 0.7 cents per play on its *paid* subscription service — less than one penny per play. And Spotify pays much less than this on its ad-supported free service. One million plays on Spotify's paid service nets the record company a few thousand dollars. One million Spotify plays will likely net the artist signed to the record company less than $1,000. If streaming cannibalizes actual record sales, most artists will make very little money from their recorded music.

For **ringtones**, phone companies pay record companies about 50% of the price charged to the phone owner for downloading the ringtone. Artists are paid by the record company an amount calculated from their base royalty rate.

Permanent downloads — meaning downloads, like iTunes, for which the digital file is permanently transferred to you — is discussed in Chapter 6. These downloads are treated like regular record sales, and artists are paid on their base royalty rate by the record company.

A record company also collects other fees from companies that use the record company's recordings in video streams, podcasts, apps, paid locker services, and bundled services. As with interactive audio streams, ringtones and permanent downloads, artists are paid by the record company an amount based on the artist's base royalty rate.

Bundled services are services sold by a company for one price, but include various services — for example, ringtones or music streaming bundled with non-musical products such as a mobile phone. A **paid locker service** is a subscription service such as iTunes cloud storage. The companies providing the service match the music you've paid for with the music they've stored in the cloud. For doing so, they pay the record company. Bundled service and paid locker providers pay over half of revenues earned from the music component of their service to the record company. Artists are paid based on their base royalty rate by the record company.

11) VIDEO STREAMING

The big three label distributors, Sony, Universal and Warner, cut deals with video streamers such as YouTube, Vevo and MTV.com that call for about a 70%/30% split of ad revenue and subscription fees generated by a video. The *songwriter's publisher* is paid from the label's share (roughly 14%-15% of the money the label receives). Artists are paid on their base royalty rate. As I write, Psy's most watched video ever *Gangnam Style* has generated over $12 million in ad revenue from YouTube, having been watched close to 2 billion times.

To appreciate the overall size of the growing music streaming market, according to Nielsen, the consumer research firm, in the first half of 2013 alone, people streamed songs over 50 billion times (combined video and audio streaming). More than 84 million of these streams were of Bruno Mars' song *When I Was Your Man*.

The following topics are covered in a typical record contract but, for now, have become less important because the industry has changed:

12) PREMIUMS

These are records sold in conjunction with other products, such as cereal. The royalty rate is typically 50% of the base rate, but the rate is not a percentage of the PPD; rather, it is a percentage of the actual price at which the record is sold to the advertiser. The artist should try to limit this type of record sale from occurring without the artist's consent.

13) RECORD CLUBS

Record clubs (like Columbia House and BMG) don't really operate anymore, but with the ever-changing music landscape, some form of record club may one day come back in a yet unanticipated form. Because the topic is still covered in most record contracts, and this could potentially harm you financially in the future, I mention it here only so that you will discuss the topic with your attorney before signing a record contract.

8. KEY RECORD CONTRACT DEAL POINTS

Now that you have a sense of the royalty numbers, the key points of a record contract discussed below will make more sense. I will not highlight issues regarding your creative freedom and control. These you already appreciate. The key points I'm going to highlight all deal, to one extent or another, with whether money ends up in the artist's pocket, or in the record company's pocket. I won't discuss each at length. Doing so would make this book far too long and would probably bore you to death. But please keep this list as a handy reference for when you are negotiating or renegotiating your record deal. Make sure you discuss each point with a good lawyer.

1) 360 DEALS

Record companies are trying to adapt their business models to the new realities facing the music business. CD sales are decreasing, and neither digital distribution of singles nor streaming is proving to be as profitable as traditional album sales. Established artists are making a larger percentage of their money from touring, and some feel no need to re-sign with a major label once their existing contracts expire. Established artists are already well known to the public. Their "brand" already exists.

New artists, or less established ones who wish to make it big in the music business, still need record labels almost as much as ever. As profits decline, labels have sought to find other ways to make money from their investments in building an artist's brand. For the most part, labels now seek to make deals whereby they profit from all sources of an artist's income — not only

from the recordings, but also from non-record sources as well —
publishing (income made by an artist as a songwriter), concerts,
merchandising, endorsements and all else. These so-called "360
deals" may or may not be the dominant contractual form of the
future because it's too soon to tell how these deals will work out,
and what the push back from talented artists might be.[24]

Nevertheless, if a new artist wants a record deal today,
he or she typically must agree to a 360 deal. In most of
these deals, the record company takes 20% to 30% of artist's
net income from all non-record sources of income. In most
instances, the artist makes his or her own deals with a publishing
company, merchandiser, tour promoter, or other entity. The
record company will not take ownership rights from the artist or
the other companies; it just takes its cut of the income.

The contractual negotiation is not only about the
percentage the record company should take of non-record
income, but also what is considered net income. Just as record
companies try to make all of their costs recoupable (i.e., charged
to the artist), in the case of net income from non-record sources,
the artist's attorney will try to lessen the net income dollars that
must be shared with the record company. Quite a dance.

1) ROYALTY RATES AND CALCULATIONS

As mentioned, an artist makes money from a record
company by receiving royalties and other payments from the
company. The more records you sell, the higher your royalty
should be. Hopefully, I have given you a good understanding of

---

[24] Interestingly, the first blockbuster deal of this nature did not involve a major label.
It was between Madonna and a concert venue owner and promoter, Live Nation — a
company that aspires to grow out of its niche. Warner Music Group was outbid.

how this works. Note that some independent labels will offer an artist a share of the profits instead of royalties if the artist is willing to forego an advance, or takes only a small advance.

Also, do carefully review any provision that calls for reduced royalty rates on "new format" records or technologies. For those who will not accept the limitations of getting music from the cloud, there will inevitably be a new format that replaces the CD as the most popular way to physically purchase music. Also, watch out for reduced royalty rate contract language on "new format" digital distribution. Don't rely on the iTunes model to always be the dominant way music is shared digitally.

2) LENGTH OF CONTRACT/OPTIONS

Generally, major labels insist that a new artist sign a contract that lasts nine months after the artist has delivered one completed album. Major label record companies also insist on receiving anywhere from three to five consecutive options to extend the term of the contract. As an artist, these options may require you to make many albums at a reduced royalty rate. Every effort should be made to limit the number of options the record company has to extend the term of your contract. The original contract should contain a clause that states the royalty payments due for each album recorded under subsequent option periods. The artist's attorney should negotiate for higher royalty rates for each new album recorded.

3) RELEASE OF THE RECORD

Just because an artist signs a record deal and makes an album does not mean that the album will be released or distributed unless the artist negotiates this into his or her contract with the record company. The release of the album should be guaranteed by the record company, or, at the very least, the contract should allow the artist to go elsewhere if the album is not released. Also, in the case of a major label, the artist will want the album released on the record company's main label, not on a smaller label that the record company just acquired or is starting.

4) PROMOTION, MARKETING & INITIAL RUN OF THE RECORD

It is critical that your record receives adequate promotion, or it will die. You should attempt to get the record company to commit to a certain dollar amount that will be spent on the promotion of your records to radio stations and music streaming services, and on the marketing of your records to stores — traditional and online. If the record company will not do so, you must question its commitment to you.

Additionally, if there is a bidding war for your services, you should attempt to get the record company to commit to hire independent promotion people on your behalf. These people are well connected with radio station programmers, but are not part of the record company's promotions department. You also want to limit how much of what a record company pays to an independent promoter is considered an advance to you, and therefore recoupable. Finally, the initial run of the record (before a record company is allowed to make the record a mid-line item) should be at least twelve months.

5) TOUR SUPPORT

Record companies want you to tour because doing so sells records (and in 360 deals, the record company participates in any profit). Unfortunately, many tours are actually money losers. I discuss this in greater detail in Chapter 19, "On Tour." If your tour is a money loser, generally 100% of the costs advanced by the record company for the tour are recoupable by the record company. Try to get the record company to guarantee tour support, at least for your first tour.

6) MERCHANDISING

As part of the 360 deals that record companies are asking new artists to sign, record companies insist on the right to sell merchandise (T-shirts, caps) with your likeness or logo on it. If you grant the record company this right (either directly, or through one of its affiliates), make sure that you actually get paid a royalty from the sale of merchandise, and that your share of the profits are not used to offset any loss the record company claims you have from record sales. I discuss this in greater detail in Chapter 20, "Selling Merchandise."

7) VIDEOS

Today, almost all record related music videos cost more money to make than they ultimately bring in, but having a video is one aspect of achieving high record sales. Videos appear less frequently on television than a few years ago, but they appear all over the internet. If you enter into a deal with a major label, it is imperative that the label provides the funds to make a good video. Exposure on YouTube is important and possibly profitable. Typically, a record company will agree to charge only 50% of the cost of making a video as recoupable against the audio (i.e., the record), but they will charge 100% of the cost of making a video as recoupable against video streaming income and the sales of videos, should there be any.

8) LIMITATIONS ON COUPLING AND COMPILATIONS

Try to limit the record company's ability to force you to participate in these arrangements. They may be good for the record company in the short run and bad for your career in the long run. *You* should have final control over your image, not the record company.

9) LIMITS ON MULTIMEDIA EXPLOITATION

Try to limit the record company's ability to license your performances without your approval. Whether it's on the internet or in the movies, you want final control over your art and image.

10) ALBUM COVER ARTWORK

Speaking of image, within the bounds of decency, whether you or the record company controls the album artwork is negotiable. This can be important for your image, and perhaps in determining to what extent you, or the record company, profit from merchandising associated with the artwork.

11) TERRITORY

For less established artists, a record company's territory is usually defined as the entire "universe." This means that the record company can sell your records anywhere. Limit a record company's territory if they are unable to effectively market your album somewhere. For instance, if you expect your music to be especially popular in Japan, it is important that the record company can effectively sell your music in Japan. As more and more records are sold outside of the U.S. and Canada, the size of a record company's territory, and your royalty rates from those territories, must be negotiated more seriously than ever before.

12) RESERVE LIMITATIONS

For physical record sales, try to negotiate the reserve percentage down. Also, try to limit the amount of time a record company can hold on to the reserve once it knows that your records were actually sold to the public. With the widespread use of Soundscan®, which tracks record sales by scanning the UPC code on the back of each record, the record companies have a pretty good idea of which albums are selling. If your records have already sold, the reserve should be reduced accordingly.

13) CONTROLLED COMPOSITION CLAUSE

In a typical record contract, the money you earn for writing songs that appear on a record is reduced if you are the artist on the record. This limitation is contained in the *controlled composition* clause of the contract. I will explain this clause in the next part of this book. You need to understand how songwriters get paid in order to fully understand it. For now, know that it is a critically important part of the artist's record deal.

14) OWNERSHIP OF THE MASTERS

Ownership of your master recordings allows your record company to exploit them. Hence, record companies wage legal wars against "free" websites. If you are a major star, you can probably insist that ownership of your masters revert to you at some point in the future. But if you are a new artist, having all your master recordings revert to you is more difficult to successfully negotiate.

Because you never know if, or when, the record company might drop you from its roster, try to negotiate to obtain ownership of *all* the masters you recorded should you and the company part ways (*including masters that were never released*). This way, should you be dropped from the label, you will be able to exploit the masters, or, at the very least, not be haunted by them when the label that dropped you releases "The Early Years" album, which will surface two years after you become a star, and will no doubt be a collection of unfinished works.

15) OWNERSHIP OF YOUR WEBSITE

Most record companies insist on the exclusive right to set up the artist's *official* website. Make sure the rights associated with the website revert to you when the term of the record contract ends.

16) ACCOUNTING AND AUDITING RIGHTS

Be sure that your contract requires a periodic accounting from the record company that details your record sales, expenses charged to your account, and royalty payments. Also, insist that the contract allows you to conduct a detailed audit of the record company's numbers. The more rights you have, the better. This can help prevent the record company from becoming sloppy with your account.

17) EXCLUSIVE RECORDING

For contracts with record companies in California, note Civil Code §3423(e) and Code of Civil Procedure §526(5), both of which deal with personal service contracts. Essentially, these code provisions deny a record company the right to obtain an injunction to stop you from recording for another company (even if you agreed to provide the record company with your exclusive services), unless the record company pays you a minimum compensation of $9,000 in the first year, $12,000 in the second year, $15,000 in the third year, and substantially more in years four through seven.

♪ ♪ ♪

Record labels are still looking for the right pricing model, and the right use allowance formula, to maximize profits from the internet. Today, singles downloads and music streaming are much less profitable than traditional album sales. The search for the right model is likely to play out over many years. For now, make sure at the very least, that your record company applies the same percentage royalty rate payable on your singles downloaded from the internet, as are payable on your regular *album* sales. In other words, your full base rate. Unfortunately, most pre-internet contracts didn't contemplate the revival of singles as a profit center, so artists with these older contracts may be paid royalties on sales of internet singles at a reduced rate.

Strive to make sure that your record contract calls for you to receive your full royalty from any new source of income that the record company receives, unless another split or royalty rate is specifically set by legal statute.

Because new unforeseen sources of artist income are inevitable from the ongoing digital revolution, make sure your lawyer covers future looking royalty and other income opportunities. Who would have expected to make money from cell phone ringtones twenty-five years ago? No one even had cell phones back then.

9. INDEPENDENT LABEL DEALS WITH MAJOR LABELS

In the past, major label record companies bought most smaller labels once they reached a certain level of success. In recent years, as record industry profits declined, many talented executives lost their jobs. This talent pool — together with the tumbling costs of recording a viable record and the exponential increase in internet download speed that enabled an alternative way of distributing music to fans — has lead to the establishment of a new crop of quality independent record labels.

There are many more labels today than there were just a few years ago. Of course, many of them are nothing more than artists' own vanity labels, yet if there is the potential for successful national distribution, a distribution deal may be struck with a major record label.

While there are *many* different types of deals entered into between independent labels and major label record companies, they tend to fall into four categories:

1) INDEPENDENT PRODUCTION AGREEMENTS

An *independent production agreement* is the agreement an independent label signs with a major label record company to manufacture, distribute, market and promote the record of an artist already signed to the independent label.

The agreement calls for the major label record company to give the independent label a 1% to 2% higher royalty rate than the major label would give on deals done directly with artists, but there is usually a cap on the total payment amount to the independent label. The more services the independent label provides by way of marketing and promoting its artist(s), the higher the royalty rate the independent can negotiate for itself. The independent retains the responsibility to pay the artist(s) their royalties.

If the major label is enamored with the owner of an independent label (e.g., a powerful record producer), or with several of the artists controlled by the independent label, an agreement covering all the artists of the independent label may be entered into.

If you are an artist, I would almost certainly advise you against signing an agreement with an independent production company that has other artists under contract unless the independent production company's deal with the major label (or the major label distributor) is structured so that you get paid royalties owed to you even if the production company is in the red with the major label vis-a-vis its other artists.

2) PROFIT-SPLITTING

Sometimes, rather than entering into an independent production agreement, the independent and major label enter into an arrangement in which the workload and profits are split between them. Under one scenario, the major label may pay for manufacturing and arrange for distribution. It would then charge the independent for all of the costs and retain a percentage of the profit. If the record is ultimately only moderately successful, it is probably economically better for the independent label to have an independent production agreement. If, however, the record is highly successful, it is better for the independent to have a profit-splitting arrangement.

3) STRAIGHT DISTRIBUTION DEALS

If an independent label wants to gamble, it may enter into a deal with a major label's distribution arm to distribute records for the independent label strictly as a wholesaler. This means that records are sold to the major distributor at a wholesale price, and the distributor marks up the wholesale price before selling it to record stores. For the most part, both physical and digital records must be part of the deal, or there will be no deal. Typically, the distribution fee is 20% to 25%.

For example, if the distributor sold a CD to a retailer for $10 (the PPD) and the distributor's fee is 25%, the distributor receives $2.50 ($10.00 x 25%) and independent label would receive $7.50 ($10.00 x 75%). For digital distribution, assuming a wholesale price of roughly $7.00 on an album priced at iTunes for $9.99, the distributor would keep $1.75 ($7.00 x 25%) and the independent label would receive $5.25 ($7.00 x 75%).

From the money the independent label receives, the independent must pay all of the manufacturing costs, overhead, artist royalties, mechanical royalties to songwriters and publishers, promotion and marketing costs, and all other costs. Whatever is left over is the independent label's profit.

4) UPSTREAM DEALS

Upstream deals are a variation of a straight distribution deal.

Over the past decades, the companies that own the major labels bought many formerly independent distributors. These once independent distributors never did, and still don't, handle marketing or promotion for the independent label. In an upstream deal, the independent label makes a deal with a major label with the understanding that one of its "independent" distributors will distribute the independent label's records. But an upstream deal gives the major label the right to move the record distribution to its major distributor.

If the major label does move the distribution to its major distributor, it will take over the functions of manufacturing, marketing and promotion of the record from the independent label. It will also take on the added risk of record returns. In exchange for taking on these added costs and risks, the profit sharing arrangement between the major label and the independent label is adjusted in the major label's favor.

BASICS FOR THE SONGWRITER

10. COPYRIGHTS — PROTECTING YOUR SONGS

Welcome to the *songwriter* section of the book. Remember, the *artist* is paid a royalty from the record company for being the performer on its record. The artist's royalty from record sales and record use is tied to income received by the record company from various sources (less a whole lot of deductions). The person who actually writes a song, *the songwriter*, makes money under different arrangements for having written the song, whether or not the songwriter is also a performing artist.

To understand how money is earned by the songwriter, you must first know a little about copyrights.

YOUR COPYRIGHT MONOPOLY

In the U.S., a copyright is a limited duration monopoly given by the government to the songwriter.[25] As the songwriter, you own a monopoly as it relates to your song. You are Mr. or Ms. Big, and you call the shots.

---

[25] Technically, the "originator" of the song gets the copyright. The originator may not be the songwriter if the songwriter agreed to write the song as a "work for hire." See the section in this chapter entitled "Works Made For Hire." This comes up most often in connection with film scores and television background music. See Chapters 22 and 23.

To obtain this copyright monopoly, the song (the "work" as it is called by the Copyright Act) has to be "original" and "of sufficient materiality." There are no specific legal tests that define what is original or what is of sufficient materiality. If there is a legal fight about whether a song is original, a judge or a jury will ultimately determine the issue based in part on their subjective views.

As soon as a "tangible" copy of your song is made, a copyright exists. A tangible copy of a song exists once you have created something you can touch, like when you burn a CD, or you create a lead sheet.[26] Technically, you don't have to file anything with the government to obtain a copyright!

Once the copyright exists, the songwriter by law is granted, among other rights, the *exclusive* rights to: 1) reproduce the work (e.g., record the song); 2) distribute copies of the work; and 3) perform the work publicly.[27] This means that no one can do any of the above without the songwriter's permission.[28] By registering a copyrighted song with the U.S. Copyright Office in Washington, D.C., the songwriter[29] can collect compulsory license royalties (discussed in the next subsection), or sue for infringement and collect the fair market value of use and the infringer's profits.[30]

---

[26] A *lead sheet* is a sheet of paper that typically contains the melody, chords and lyrics of a song.

[27] Further rights are listed in §106 of the Copyright Act of 1976.

[28] Congress continues to hold hearings to determine the best way to protect copyrights in an age of digital transmission. Existing copyright laws don't adequately deal with issues surrounding newer technology. Until laws are written to settle matters, expect to see ongoing litigation.

[29] Your publisher may be the one registering the copyright with the Copyright Office if you have transferred copyright ownership to your publisher.

Infringement

It is considered illegal *infringement* for a songwriter to use a portion of someone else's copyrighted song in a new song without permission unless the new song only includes "fair use" of the copyrighted song. Whether a particular use of a portion of someone else's song constitutes "fair use" depends on a number of factors, including how much of the copyrighted song is used, in what context it is used, and whether the use of the copyrighted song will deprive the copyright owner of future profits. On occasion, parody may be considered fair use. If you are going to use any part of an older song in your song, obtain permission to do so. Don't rely on the narrow fair use defense.

Obviously, infringement of an existing song defeats copyright protection in the newer song. If it can be shown that the person who claims authorship of a new song had "access"[31] to the older song, (e.g., you heard it on the radio) the remaining legal test is simply whether the amount taken from the older copyrighted song (music or words) was "substantial." This loose standard is applied by the judge or jury when listening to the songs and comparing them.

---

[30] Legal issues surrounding copyright infringement can be complex, with many such issues still being decided by the courts. "Sampling" (i.e., digitally recording a small portion of an existing song), for example, is currently determined by a fairly open-ended standard: if the sound sampled was so distinctive and unusual to be thought of by a judge or a jury as "original," anyone who samples the sound and uses the sample as part of a new song may be guilty of infringement. There are firms, such as EMG Music Clearance and Parker Music Group, that specialize in obtaining copyright clearances so that you can legally sample someone else's work.

[31] "Access" in the context of infringement is a legal term of art. Access can be shown if a person heard or had knowledge of someone else's work, or had a reasonable opportunity to hear or view the work.

Joint Works

Joint works are songs written by two or more people. If two or more songwriters intend to merge their individual contribution at the time of a song's creation, the writers have created a *joint-work*. Each songwriter has the right to license the entire song, subject to paying the other songwriter(s) their share of the royalties, because each owns an undivided interest in the copyright of the entire song.[32]

Even if the writers create separate parts, as when one writes the music and the other writes the lyrics, each is a co-owner of the indivisible whole of the joint work. If, for example, the original lyrics are later completely rejected and a new songwriter writes new lyrics, the original lyricist still owns a part of the new song! This new song is called a *derivative work*.[33]

If you want to avoid having someone claim that his contribution to your song was intended to create a joint work, make it clear up front. You do not want any other person claiming an interest in your copyright. For instance, when you are making a demo with the help of a producer or arranger, always clarify that his or her services are being rendered as a producer or arranger, and not as a songwriter.

---

[32] This is discussed in §201(a) of the Copyright Act of 1976.

[33] Technically, a derivative work is a song (or other "work") that is created by the making of modifications or additions to a preexisting work. In the example above, the original lyrics and melody form the preexisting work, while the new songwriter's lyrics together with the original melody comprise the derivative work. If the original lyricist uses the original lyrics with a new melody, it too is a "derivative work."

Arrangements

Arrangements of songs seldom qualify for copyright protection. Under the Copyright Act, arrangements are copyrightable if the arrangement was made by the copyright owner of the song, or the copyright owner of the song consents to allowing the arrangement to be copyrighted. Otherwise, the arrangement itself must be found to be "original" and "of sufficient materiality," not simply an expression of your underlying idea. So, just because your song is recorded in someone else's studio, and the studio owner helps you produce or arrange your song by adding key instrumental tracks and helping you phrase the song just right, does not mean that he or she is entitled to a copyrightable interest in either your song or the arrangement of your song.

Works Made For Hire

Works made for hire, also known as *works for hire*, refers to songs written by a songwriter either as an employee or as an independent contractor for someone else. **The person or entity who does the hiring — not the actual songwriter — is the *originator* and *author* of the song, and therefore owns the copyright.**[34] The royalties generated by a song belong to the employer, not to the actual songwriter, unless the work for hire agreement specifically grants the songwriter an interest in royalty income.

---

[34] To meet the requirements of the copyright act, a work for hire contract must be in writing. In other words, you cannot legally enter into a work for hire contract that is not in writing. See §201(b) of the Copyright Act of 1976.

EXCEPTIONS TO YOUR COPYRIGHT MONOPOLY

There are several exceptions under the Copyright Act to a songwriter's exclusive monopoly rights. The most important one involves the use of a song on a record.

A license to use the song *must* be granted by the copyright owner if all of the following are true: 1) the song is a "nondramatic" musical composition;[35] 2) the song has been previously recorded and distributed publicly in "phonorecords" with the copyright owner's permission;[36] and 3) the requested license is for the use of your song in phonorecords only.

The license that must be granted if all of the above is true is referred to as a ***compulsory mechanical license,*** and is the major basis upon which payment by record companies to songwriters and publishers is calculated. If a record company wants to take advantage of a compulsory mechanical license to use your song, it must pay you a royalty in exchange for it.

Note that there is *no* compulsory license for songs used in movies, video games, DVDs or video streaming websites such as YouTube. If you do not want your song to be used in a movie or on YouTube, it can't be used.[37] For the right to use your song in

---

[35] The law does not give the words "dramatic musical composition" clear meaning. You can assume that your song is a "nondramatic musical composition," unless it is written specifically for a musical or an opera. However, even if your song is written for a musical or an opera, it might still be considered a "nondramatic musical composition" if it is later used in a nondramatic fashion (e.g., played on the radio).

[36] Pursuant to the Copyright Act, "phonorecord" means every form of recording (CDs, tapes, mp3 files stored on a computer, etc.) except recordings "accompanying a motion picture or other audiovisual work." Specifically included in the definition of "phonorecord" is digital phonorecord delivery (i.e., digital downloads.)

a movie, you are free to charge a film company whatever you want (or whatever it is willing to pay).

THE COPYRIGHT NOTICE

Legally, in the U.S., you don't have to put any copyright notice on songs first "published" on or after March 1, 1989.[38] But, giving notice does serve to inform others that the song is yours, and also allows for certain benefits in a court of law should someone infringe on your song. Though not required, I also recommend that you place a copyright notice on your demos. It appears more professional. The symbol for a notice of copyright in a song is ©, and the symbol for a notice of copyright in a sound recording is ℗. Here's how you place a copyright notice:

If you are protecting anything that is "visibly perceptible" (i.e., you can see it), use the symbol ©. You should use this symbol on lead sheets, J-cards, sheet music and albums (if lyrics are printed and to protect the artwork). For example, on my lead sheets, I would put: **© 2013 David Naggar**

If you are protecting the sound recording itself (which is not visibly perceptible), use the symbol ℗. Put this notice on the surface, label or container of the CD or other audio file. If your CD, DVD, or other music container has artwork that you wish to protect, add the symbol ©. On my CD I would put:
℗ © 2013 David Naggar

---

[37] Other compulsory licenses involve cable television, public television (PBS) and jukeboxes. There are also compulsory license requirements for certain digital transmissions of sound recordings pursuant to the Digital Performance Right in Sound Recordings Act of 1995, and the Digital Millennium Copyright Act.

[38] "Publication" is defined by the Copyright Act as "the distribution of copies of phonorecords of a work to the public by sale or other transfer of ownership, or by rental, lease, or lending."

For a copyright notice to be effective in the U.S., you must include: 1) the letter C or P inside a circle;[39] 2) the year of publication (publication generally occurs when the song is distributed to the public); and 3) the name(s) of the copyright owner(s). All three must be included.

COPYRIGHT REGISTRATION FORMS

Although material can be protected by simply using the © or ℗ symbols, in order to collect compulsory license royalties or sue for infringement, a copyright must also be registered with the U.S. Copyright Office. The fee is $65 per registration ($35 if you register online), but you can register a collection of your songs as one "work" and save a lot of money. If you don't want to register your copyright online, you can download the necessary forms at www.copyright.gov, or call the Copyright Office at (202) 707-3000 to have the forms mailed to you. You'll need form PA — *for Performing Arts* — if you want to register a song only, and form SR — *for Sound Recording* — if you want to register both the song *and* a recording at the same time.

THE DURATION OF A COPYRIGHT

A copyright for works created after January 1, 1978 is valid in the U.S. for the life of the last surviving author plus 70 years.

Copyright protection for works first published and registered with the Copyright Office between January 1, 1964 and December 31, 1977 is valid initially for 28 years. There is an automatic renewal of the copyright protection for an additional

---

[39] You can also use the word copyright or copr. instead of the letter C inside a circle.

67 years at the expiration of the 28-year period.[40] Thus, the total copyright protection is 95 years from the date of publication.

U.S. copyright protection for all works published before January 1, 1964 has either expired (which means that the works are in the public domain and anyone can use them for free),[41] or has already been properly extended with the Copyright Office (which means that the copyright is valid for 95 years from the date of publication).[42] Anyone can freely use any song in the U.S. which was registered by an American author before 1923,[43] and any work registered by an American author between 1923 and 1963 for which a proper application to extend copyright protection was not filed with the Copyright Office.

Now that you know how to protect your songs, let's discuss sending out your demos.

♪ ♪ ♪

---

[40] Because of burden of proof issues that arise in a court of law, and because of issues relating to derivative works, it is better practice to actually file a renewal notice.

[41] Once a song is in the public domain, the copyright owner is no longer entitled to any royalty payment.

[42] The duration of a copyright on works for hire is the lesser of 95 years from publication or 120 years from creation.

[43] The Sony Bono Copyright Term Extension Act, which became law in 1998, extended the life of a copyright in the U.S. by 20 years for songs registered in 1923 and thereafter. In other words, the copyright used to last for the life of the author plus 50 years. Older works had 75 years, not 95 years of protection. Songs registered by American authors in 1922 and before did not benefit from this extra 20 years of protection and have fallen into the public domain, at least for use in the U.S. Because of an international agreement entered into in 1994 (the General Agreement on Tariffs and Trade (GATT)), foreign works first published abroad before 1923 may in certain situations retain copyright protection in the U.S. for 95 year from when first registered.

11. SENDING OUT YOUR SONGS

Leaving art aside, as a songwriter, your primary goal is to get your songs on a record.

If you do not have an active publisher, material you send directly to anybody who can actually help you earn money from your song (including a publisher) will generally not be listened to no matter how good it is, unless it is first solicited. People in the business are afraid to be the target of lawsuits by songwriters who later claim that their words or music were stolen and used in another song.

Initially, it is best to have someone in the business end of the music industry, such as a music attorney, send out your material because it lends more credibility to your songs. A great song can, however, occasionally speak for itself, even if it does come directly from you.

If you do send out your own song demo CDs, mp3 files, or a website link, send them to those who are as close to the decision-making source as possible! If an artist is established, the artist, his or her personal manager, or the producer of the artist's last album, is *much* more likely than the publisher or an A & R rep to ultimately decide what goes on the artist's record.

If, on the other hand, an artist is newly signed, and not widely known, the record company may dictate which songs ultimately appear on the artist's record. Remember though, if you haven't received permission to send your demo, it probably won't be listened to by anybody. Here are two of the better sources to help a songwriter send a demo to the right place. Unfortunately, to get your hands on either of them will cost over $100:

1) Pollstar

POLLSTAR USA, 4697 W. Jacquelyn Ave., Fresno, CA 93722; tel. (559) 271-7900; www.pollstar.com. POLLSTAR concentrates on providing concert tour information, but subscribers also receive "Contact Directories," which include record company rosters, music radio directories and agency directories. The Contact Directory most valuable to you, the songwriter, is the one directory not included in the cost of the subscription, the "Artist Management Directory." The Roster gives current contact information for artists' managers. It currently sells for $149.95.

2) Billboard

Billboard's International Talent & Touring Directory, published annually, lists hundreds of artists, together with booking agents, personal managers and record companies. There is also a section on where to contact the agents and managers. Billboard Directories, P.O. Box 15158, North Hollywood, CA 91606; tel. (800) 562-2706; www.orderbillboard.com.

PUBLISHER AND A & R NAMES

The Music Registry is a *great* source of industry names (but not for artist and artist management contact information). There are four registries that list contact information for music business players: 1) an A & R directory; 2) a music publishers directory; 3) a legal and business affairs directory; and 4) a film and television music directory. The Music Business Registry, Inc., 7510 Sunset Blvd., Suite 1041, Los Angeles CA 90046; tel. (800) 377-7411; www.musicregistry.com.

If you already know the name of a company, or the name of a person in the industry, All Access Music Group has a database that allows you to search over 100,000 listings for free. www.allaccess.com/industry-directory.

♪ ♪ ♪

Also, important who's who tidbits can often be found in the major industry trade magazine, *Billboard*. Other good sources of information are *The Musician's Atlas*, which lists many industry contacts, and *Hits Magazine Online - Hits Daily Double*.

12. PRIMARY SOURCES OF INCOME

A songwriter makes money by selling — generally through his or her publisher — rights to use one or more of the songwriter's songs. In most circumstances, in order to get paid, a publishing entity that owns the legal copyright to the song must be specified. A songwriter may act as his or her own publisher. (See Chapter 16, "Creating Your Own Publishing Company.") However, the songwriter can often generate substantially more income from a song by associating with a major publishing company.

Profits generated from a song are split between the songwriter and the publisher (even if you act as your own publisher). Through quirks of history, the holder(s) of the *publisher's share* (regardless of who owns "the publishing" — i.e., the copyright rights) are generally said to receive 50% of the song's profits. The remaining 50% is said to be the *writer's share*. Notwithstanding the use of the terms *publisher's share* and *writer's share*, the actual profits split between a songwriter and a "real" publisher vary greatly depending on the arrangement between them. Very often, the songwriter receives a large portion of the *publisher's share*. Therefore, in this chapter I will discuss the total money generated by a song. I will discuss the role of publishers in more detail in Chapter 14.

The two primary sources of income for songs are: 1) *mechanical* **royalties paid by the record company for using the songwriter's song on one of its records; and 2)** *performing* **royalties paid by television stations, radio stations, satellite radio stations, online streaming services, night clubs, restaurants,**

and others for playing the songwriter's song publicly. Note that *performing* royalties are not paid by artists for performing a song, though technically, an artist could be held accountable to make such a payment.

1) MECHANICAL ROYALTIES

In exchange for mechanical rights to reproduce copies of a song in records, record companies pay mechanical royalties to the copyright owner of a song. The copyright owner is the songwriter or any person or entity to which the songwriter assigns the legal copyright ownership.

The amount of the payment is typically negotiated between the record company and the copyright owner. However, if the criteria discussed in the "Exceptions To Your Copyright Monopoly" section of Chapter 10 are met, a copyright owner *must* license his or her song to any record company that agrees to pay the compulsory mechanical license rate set by statute.[44] Currently, the rate per song is the larger of 1) 9.1¢, or 2) 1.75¢ per minute of playing time (or fraction thereof) for each record sold.[45]

For example, if your 3-minute song was licensed to a record company under the terms of a *compulsory* mechanical license for use on an album that sold 100,000 copies, a record company would be obligated to pay the copyright owner $9,100 (100,000 x 9.1¢) in mechanical royalties.

---

[44] The rate is set by three administrative judges — the Copyright Royalty Board.

[45] A song lasting five minutes and one second is considered to be a six minute song for purposes of the payment calculation.

If your six-and-a-half-minute song was licensed to a record company under the terms of a compulsory mechanical license for use on an album that sold 2,000,000 copies, a record company would be obligated to pay the copyright owner $245,000 (2,000,000 x 1.75¢ x 7) in mechanical royalties.

If you co-wrote four 3-minute songs with a friend, and each of the songs was licensed to a record company under the terms of a compulsory mechanical license for use on an album that sold 500,000 copies (a gold album), a record company would be obligated to pay the copyright owners $182,000 (500,000 x 4 songs x 9.1¢) in mechanical royalties. Assuming you and your friend agreed to a 50/50 split on income from songs written together, you and your publisher would receive $91,000 (half of the $182,000). Your friend (and his or her publisher) would receive the other half.[46]

Of course, record companies do not want to pay the full statutory amount, and so, they attempt to negotiate agreements with copyright owners that call for payment of a reduced rate. If, however, a record company does not agree to pay the full statutory amount, the copyright owner can refuse to allow the record company to use the song.

The predominant way in which a record company forces a reduction in the amount of mechanical royalties it has to pay a songwriter is contained in the so-called *controlled composition*

---

[46] Compulsory mechanical licenses are hardly ever used! It is easier for a copyright owner to monitor direct licenses. It is also easier for record companies to deal with direct licenses because the compulsory accounting rules are considered too time-consuming. The statutory compulsory mechanical license rate is important because it sets the standard for the mechanical rates that record companies actually do pay.

clause of a record contract between the *artist* and the record company.

A *controlled composition* is a song written, owned or controlled, in whole or in part, by the artist. Since, unlike artist royalties, the record company cannot recoup money from a *songwriter's* mechanical royalties,[47] record companies typically insist that the artist (with the exception of major stars) agree to license songs controlled by the artist for 75% of the minimum statutory rate. In other words, no matter how long the song is, the record company will pay only 6.825¢ (75% x 9.1¢).[48] Often, record companies pay only 4.55¢ (50% x 9.1¢) for mid-line and budget records. Also, the controlled composition clause will often limit the record company's total mechanical royalty payments on any album to one of the following: 1) the number of songs actually on the album x 6.825¢ (75% of the statutory rate); 2) 81.9¢ (12 x 6.825¢); or 3) 68.25¢ (10 x 6.825¢), depending on the artist's negotiating strength.[49]

If an artist uses songs on an album from an outside songwriter (i.e., a non-controlled composition) and the outside songwriter insists on getting the full statutory amount (9.1¢), then the artist is very likely to end up receiving less than 75% of 9.1¢ on the songs the artist *has* written. The artist will receive, as income earned in his or her capacity as a songwriter,

---

[47] Money isn't "advanced" by the record company to the songwriter in the same way it is advanced to the artist.

[48] Any record contract entered into after June 22, 1995 must include the full statutory rate payment for digital downloads, regardless of a controlled composition clause.

[49] Also, the record company will insist that no mechanical royalties on controlled compositions be paid on "free goods."

only what is left over from the mechanical royalty payment pie allotted for *all* the songs written for the entire album. If a typical controlled composition clause is included as part of the record contract, mechanical royalties paid by the record company in excess of 81.9¢ or 68.25¢ per album, depending on the deal, may be charged as an advance against the artist's other royalties. This is complicated but important to know, because if an artist puts a song from an outside songwriter on the album, it can hurt the artist financially. And, if the artist does not think that putting the outside songwriter's song on the album will make the artist more money than if the song was not on the album, the song won't be there.

Here's an example: Suppose an artist's deal with the record company states that mechanical royalties paid in excess of 68.25¢ per album will be charged as an advance against the artist's other royalties. Also, for purposes of this example, assume there are 12 songs on the album — 6 written by the artist, and 6 written by an outside songwriter who insists on receiving the full statutory mechanical royalty rate of 9.1¢.

Six outside songwriter songs (9.1¢ x 6)	54.60¢
Six songs written by artist (75% x 9.1¢ x 6)	+40.95¢
Total mechanical royalties payable by record company per album	95.55¢
Less: Per album mechanical pie (as agreed to in the artist's record contract)	− 68.25¢
Amount payable in excess of album mechanical pie (charged as an advance against artist's other royalties)	= 27.30¢
Net amount per album artist will actually receive for writing six songs on the album (40.95¢ minus 27.30¢)	13.65¢

As you can see, the business reality of the controlled composition clause often forces all but the most sought after outside songwriters to accept a reduced mechanical royalty rate equal to 6.825¢ per song. Even sought after songwriters often accept a reduced mechanical royalty rate of 6.825¢ for sales of mid-line or budget records.[50]

2) PERFORMING ROYALTIES

Television stations, am/fm and satellite radio stations, podcasters, night clubs and other public users of music, such as companies that provide elevator music, pay performing royalties in exchange for the right to play songs in public.

Until a few years ago, *every* nightclub, restaurant and other place you heard music publicly was charged a fee.[51] Since it would be too cumbersome for every public user of music to enter into a separate royalty agreement with each copyright owner of music, *performance rights societies* that represent the interests of songwriters and their publishers have come into existence.[52]

---

[50] Canada has its own rates, but are generally economically tied to the U.S. rates. Except for the U.S. and Canada, most countries have entirely different copyright royalty systems. "Mechanicals" in most other countries are a set percentage of the wholesale price of the record, even if the record contains multiple songs on it.

[51] As part of the Sony Bono Copyright Term Extension Act, under certain circumstances, restaurants and bars of less than 3,750 sq. ft. and retail stores of less than 2,000 sq. ft. don't have to pay a fee. However, the World Trade Organization has ruled that this law violates U.S. international copyright obligations to the European Union (EU). For now, the U.S. is compensating the EU for this violation, but ultimately the EU is pushing the U.S. to change its law.

[52] For political reasons, performance rights societies do not collect royalties for music performed in films playing in U.S. theaters.

Songwriters and their publishers affiliate independently with a performance rights society.[53] In the U.S., ASCAP and BMI are the dominant performance rights societies.[54] Both are non-profit organizations. Other countries have their equivalent societies.

For each public user of music, each society negotiates a separate licensing agreement. For a negotiated set fee, most of the licensing agreements allow the public user to use all of the songs of all the copyright owners the society represents.

The society collects the *performing* royalties from each public user, deducts the society's expenses (about 11%-13% of the money collected), and distributes the remainder to its songwriter and publisher members. Of the amount distributed, the songwriter members receive 50% and the publisher members receive 50%. Unlike *mechanical royalties* that record companies pay entirely to publishers (who then pay songwriters their agreed share), the performance rights societies directly pay affiliated songwriter members 50% (in addition to directly paying the publisher members 50%). As an individual songwriter, you may be entitled to part of the publisher's share of performing royalties (depending on your deal with your publisher), but these royalties will need to be collected from the publisher after the performance rights society pays the publisher.

---

[53] As a songwriter, you can be affiliated with only one society at any given time, and, generally, your application will not be accepted by a society unless you have a song on a record that is, or will soon be, sold publicly. If a songwriter acts as his or her own publisher, a separate affiliation, as a publisher, is required.

[54] SESAC is the other performance rights society in the United States. SESAC, however, only controls a small percentage of U.S. performing rights. For clarity, I have limited my discussion to ASCAP and BMI, but the information given also applies to SESAC (with the exception that SESAC is actually a for-profit organization).

Allocation Of Royalty License Proceeds Among The Society's Members

Both ASCAP and BMI take in hundreds of millions of dollars in receipts each year. By far the largest sources of income are television and radio. For most performances of music, ASCAP and BMI pay songwriter and publisher members quarterly (i.e., four times a year). Payment occurs about six months after the end of the three month period in which the performing monies were earned.

These societies use very different methods of calculating which songs, and which songwriter members, are entitled to what percentage of the income that will ultimately be distributed to the various songwriters.[55] Because each songwriter's situation is unique, it is difficult to say which society pays its songwriters more in any given year. Once it becomes generally known that one society is paying a bit more than the other, the payments tend to equalize. Therefore, which society will ultimately be more beneficial to a new songwriter cannot be said with any degree of certainty. But both of these societies work on behalf of songwriters and publishers. Their purpose is not to rip you off.

To give you a rough idea of the dollars involved, the number one *Billboard* pop song of the year can earn the songwriter and publisher $2,000,000 (50% of this amount will be paid directly to the songwriter member(s) who wrote the song, and 50% will be paid to the publisher member(s) who published the song). If a pop song reaches number one, it is likely to be

---

[55] Descriptions of the various factors and formulas that determine the actual payment to songwriters can be found at the ASCAP and BMI websites: www.ascap.com and www.bmi.com, respectively.

played publicly enough times to generate over $750,000.

If a song only reaches number 50, it is likely to be played publicly enough times to generate a little under $100,000 in performing royalties for the songwriter and publisher.

And then there are television commercials. A hit song used in a commercial that has a two-year run can generate over $500,000 for the songwriter and publisher.

As mentioned earlier, a songwriter may be entitled to part of his or her publisher's share of performing royalties, but these royalties will need to be collected from the publisher directly, not from the performance rights society.

♪ ♪ ♪

Technology sometimes moves faster than the law. In the case of music streaming technology, technically the music you hear ought be subject to *both* a mechanical royalty and a performing royalty payment to the publisher/songwriter — a mechanical royalty because the music must first be copied to a server before it can be streamed, and a performing royalty because the music is being listened to without the listener owning a copy of the music.

Because publishers are responsible for collecting mechanical royalties, but performance rights societies are responsible for collecting performing royalties, there is also a bit of a turf war going on over who gets to collect the royalties (and charge for doing so).

In the United States, ringtones and permanent downloads — like from iTunes — are treated as mechanical uses, subject to mechanical royalties. Satellite Radio and non-interactive webcasting (where the user isn't choosing what song to listen to) are treated as performances, subject to performing royalties that ASCAP, BMI and SESAC (the other, much smaller, performance rights society in the United States) collect for the publisher and songwriter.

Interactive audio streaming on demand — where the listener chooses what song to listen to — are subject to both mechanical and performing royalties.[56]

---

[56] The rate formulas for determining limited download and interactive streaming rates were agreed to by publisher and record company representatives and approved by the Copyright Royalty Board. These rate formulas can be found at 37 CFR §385.10 through §385.17 (See also footnote 57). Proposed rate formulas for Mixed Service Bundles, Music Bundles, Limited Offerings (non-interactive services), paid locker services and purchased content lockers (free lockers) will likely be in effect by the time you read this and will probably be found at 37 CFR §385.21.

13. SECONDARY SOURCES OF INCOME

LIMITED DOWNLOAD AND INTERACTIVE STREAMING LICENSES

Songwriters get paid by record companies for songs downloaded and permanently licensed to the music buyer, such as songs downloaded from iTunes. The statutory mechanical rate payable to the songwriter's publisher (as owner of the rights to the song) for this type of download, a ***non-limited*** *download*, is the same 9.1¢ as for any other use of a song on a record.

But when a download is "***limited***," that is, not permanently licensed to the music fan, *or*, when the music fan is free to decide what song to hear, and when to hear it (i.e., music streaming on demand), the statutory rates vary. The rates depend on the exact music service being offered.[57] This is the world of subscription services such as Rhapsody and Rdio, but also includes sites such as iTunes Radio, Pandora and Spotify that offer music streaming without a subscription. Traditional copyright laws are difficult to properly apply to the reality of the web and digital transmission.

---

[57] The statutory rate structure is complicated, but generally can be thought of as the *greater of* 1) 10.5% of the subscription revenue (or the gross advertising revenue, less some costs associated with getting the ads); 2) a defined user fee per subscriber that ranges from 15¢ to 50¢, depending on the service offered; and 3) 17.36% to 18% of the fee paid by a service provider to a record company for use of the master recording and publishing combined, or if the service provider pays the publisher directly, 21% to 22% of the fee the service provider paid to the record company for use of the master recording alone. Finally, subtracted from the dollar amount this calculation renders, is the amount paid to ASCAP/BMI/SESAC as the publisher/songwriter share of performing royalties. The exact categories of users, and the license fees associated with each, can be found at www.harryfox.com. I'll talk about the Harry Fox Agency in the next Chapter, Chapter 14.

FOREIGN MECHANICAL RIGHTS

Foreign royalties are becoming a larger percentage of the songwriter's profit picture as sales of U.S. artists' records grow internationally.

Most countries have mechanical rights collection organizations that license all musical compositions. Unlike the U.S., where mechanical licenses are based on a statutory rate per song, the mechanical amount collected in most foreign countries is based on a percentage of the wholesale price of a record, even if the record contains multiple songs on it. Foreign publishers are generally contracted to collect royalty monies earned in other countries because they are more aware of the nuances particular to a local country. Foreign publishers acting in this capacity are referred to as *sub-publishers* because they are accountable in the performance of their duties to the U.S. publisher.

FOREIGN PERFORMING RIGHTS

Almost every country has its own equivalent of ASCAP and BMI. Both ASCAP and BMI enter into contracts with these societies to collect monies for their own ASCAP or BMI affiliated **songwriters**, respectively. A little over 25% of all performing monies received by ASCAP and BMI come from foreign societies, and this percentage is increasing rapidly.

Generally, large **publishers** contract with foreign sub-publishers to collect the publisher's share of foreign performing royalties from each country's performing rights society because payment is much quicker than if the publisher contracted with the foreign performing rights societies directly. In a typical sub-publisher deal, the sub-publisher keeps

15% to 25% of the monies earned.

SYNCHRONIZATION LICENSE FEES

Companies, such as those producing television shows, movies, advertisements, DVDs, and websites that wish to synchronize a songwriter's music to their visual images, must obtain a **synchronization ("sync") license** to do so. But remember, a songwriter does not have to license the use of his or her songs to these users. There is no compulsory requirement to do so. That is why these fees are fluid and depend greatly on the perceived importance of the song to the visual images.

As an example, for use in a major advertisement campaign on national television, a well-known song can earn from $50,000 to well over $1,000,000. The same song can earn up to $250,000 if used in a major film. And typically, the song will earn $10,000 to $20,000 if used in a network television episode that contractually may be shown forever around the globe, but less than $3,500 if used in a non-network television episode that contractually may be shown worldwide for only five or six years.

The sync license fees for television are lower than those for film because 1) television budgets are lower; 2) television reaches a much wider audience and therefore reaches more potential record buyers; and 3) a song used on television will generate extra performing royalties.

Video streaming websites like YouTube, Vevo and MTV.com also must pay a sync license fee to use a songwriter's song, or they can't use it. The three big record label distributors, Sony, Universal and Warner cut deals with video streamers that call for about a 70%/30% split of ad revenue and subscription fees generated by a video. The songwriter's publisher is paid from the label's share (roughly 14%-15% of the money the label receives). For songwriters whose songs aren't connected to the big labels, YouTube will pay up to 50% of ad revenues to the publisher.

App makers who use songs in their apps must also pay sync license fees, as do podcasters for podcasting songs. The sync license fees for use of music in an app and other multimedia sources such as exercise DVDs and video games can be all over the board, as I will discuss in Chapter 25.

OTHER DIGITAL MECHANICAL LICENSES

Ringtones — The statutory mechanical rate paid to the songwriter/publisher when someone downloads part of their song for use as a ringtone is 24¢.

Bundled services — Mechanical royalties are paid on two kinds of bundled services: **mixed service bundles**, and **music bundles**. Mixed services bundles are services that are sold by a company for one price, but include various services — for example, ringtones or music streaming bundled with non-musical products such as a mobile phone or internet access, all for one price. Music Bundles are bundles that might include a CD and a copy of a digital download. In other words, music only bundles.

Locker services — Mechanical royalties are also paid on two kinds of locker services: **paid locker services** and **purchased content locker services** (free lockers). A paid locker service is a subscription service such as iTunes cloud storage. The service provider matches the music you've paid for with the music they've stored in the cloud. A purchased content locker service is free cloud storage for a user's digital music files — files the user already downloaded and paid for.

SHEET MUSIC

The royalty paid by a sheet music company is typically 20% of the retail selling price for sheet music containing a single song. Today, this equals about 80¢ to 99¢ (20% of $3.99 to $4.95 — the typical retail price of sheet music).[58]

Folios are collections of songs. The total royalty paid by sheet music companies for the songs included in a folio ranges from 10% to 12.5% of the retail selling price of the folio. Folios can be "mixed," "matching" or "personality" folios. A "mixed folio" is a collection of well-known songs made popular by various artists. A "matching folio" is a collection of songs from a particular album. "Personality folios" are those that have the artist's picture on the cover. In personality folios, in addition to money paid to the publisher/songwriter, a 5% royalty is typically paid to the artist (for the use of the songs as well as the artist's name and likeness). *Instructional print music* (e.g., "How to play the piano" folios) bears a 10% royalty payment.[59]

---

[58] As the global economy takes stronger root, more and more major publishing companies are able to receive 20% of the retail selling price on sheet music sold outside of the U.S. and Canada as well.

[59] There are four major manufactures of secular printed music in the U.S.: Alfred Music, BMG Rights Management, Hal Leonard Corp., and Music Sales Corp.

14. MUSIC PUBLISHING

PUBLISHERS

If you are like most artists and songwriters, you probably wonder what exactly publishers do and why so many people who haven't yet profited financially from their art tell you to "hang on to your publishing."

There is a lot more to publishing than filling out ASCAP/BMI forms and copyright registration forms. Full-service publishing companies find artists, record companies, film companies, television production companies, advertisers, producers of video games and DVDs, web companies, and others to use a songwriter's song. They negotiate licenses with anyone using the song, and ensure that proper fees are paid. They also monitor the song's public usage to make sure it is properly reported to the performance rights society. Doing so ensures that performing royalties are not lost. In short, a good full-service publisher may generate more income from a song than the songwriter could, and also, the songwriter's time is freed up to write new songs.

Typically, in exchange for doing all of the above for the songwriter, a publisher insists that the songwriter transfer all of his or her official copyright "rights" to the publisher. The publisher and the songwriter then split the profits generated by the song. Review the "Your Copyright Monopoly" section of Chapter 10 for a refresher on the rights the publisher wants you to transfer.

Historically, the publisher received 50% of the song's profits. Over time, as the record industry has matured, the role of publishers has become less important. Many artists now write their own songs and act as their own publishers. Other well-known songwriters do not need someone to find a recording artist for them; to the contrary, the artists seek them out. So today, for successful songwriters with an established track record, major publishing companies are, in essence, little more than paperwork/financing companies, advancing the songwriters money in exchange for anticipated profits from a song. The songwriter receives a steady income, and the publisher and songwriter agree to split the publishing share of income.

If, for example, the songwriter and publishing company agree to split *the publishing* 50%/50%, then the songwriter retains 75% of the profits earned from the song (100% of the songwriter's share of profits, and 50% of the publisher's share of profits).

Nevertheless, as I mentioned earlier, through quirks of history, the holder(s) of the **publisher's share** (regardless of who owns the "publishing" — i.e., the copyright rights) are generally said to receive 50% of the song's profits. The remaining 50% is said to be the **writer's share**. This is why the songwriter receives 50% of the performing royalties (i.e., the writer's share) directly from ASCAP or BMI. Even if the songwriter has a contract with a publishing company that states that the songwriter is retaining an interest in the publisher's share, the full publisher's share of performing royalties is generally paid by ASCAP or BMI directly to the major publishing company. It is up to the songwriter to make sure the publishing company pays the songwriter his or her portion of the retained publisher's share.[60]

---

[60] ASCAP and BMI will not typically make payments directly to a publishing company that is created by the writer for the express purpose of sharing the "publishing" with a major publishing company.

A major publishing company has many departments to ensure that the publisher's entire operation runs smoothly. The publisher's paperwork (e.g., registering songs with the copyright office, issuing licenses, making sure the correct amount of royalties are being paid for the songs and disbursed to the writers) is handled by a combination of departments including what are often called the Business/Legal Affairs Department, the Copyright Department and the Royalties Department. Placing the publisher's songs with users, finding new songwriters, and helping the songwriter improve the songwriter's songs so that the publisher has better songs to sell, are all handled by what is typically called the Creative Department.

Universal Music Group bought BMG in 2007 to become the largest music publisher in the world. Warner/Chappell and Sony/ATV (which bought EMI's large publishing catalogue in 2012) are also industry heavyweights. These three companies each own the rights to, and have to keep track of, literally hundreds of thousands of songs. Every time you hear the song "Happy Birthday" in a movie or on television, Warner/Chappell makes money. (Wouldn't you love to own the rights to that song?)

However, because becoming a publishing company is not as capital intensive as becoming a successful record company, the publishing industry is not dominated by publishing companies the way the record industry is dominated by the majors.

Essentially, there are only two key parts to a publishing company:

Administrative — to take care of the paperwork.
Creative—to find the writers, to help improve their songs and to run around schmoozing people in order to get songs recorded or used in movies and television.

That is why a publishing company does not have to be big to be successful. A song on a record label that lacks sufficient market presence and financial backing is unlikely to be widely heard, no matter how great the song is. A publishing company does not require the financial backing that a record company does. A publisher need only enter into a mechanical licensing agreement with a record company to place a song as a single or on an album. The marketing and promotion of the single or the album will be financially supported by the record company.

You may have heard of the Harry Fox Agency. The Harry Fox Agency is a part of the National Music Publishers Association that issues mechanical licenses for most publishers in the U.S., ensures that mechanical royalties are paid, and accounts to the publishers. They also perform occasional audits of the record companies to make sure the correct amount of mechanical royalties is being paid. For its services, the Harry Fox Agency charges 6.75% of the royalties distributed. It has particularly useful information about issuing mechanical licenses in the FAQ (frequently asked questions) link at its website: www.harryfox.com.

SONGWRITER DEALS WITH PUBLISHERS

When you are entering into a contract to give up part of your publishing, make sure the publisher is providing you with a service you anticipate will generate more money to you than you would otherwise receive if you did not do the deal. If you do not believe that a particular publisher will make you money, do not enter into the contract!

There may be any number of reasons to have someone else handle your publishing. You may not want to do your own administrative paperwork. (It's a pain to do.) You may not have the contacts to get your song(s) to artists and other users of music, or, you may not be able to get an independent label to take you on as an artist unless you offset some of its risk by including some of your publishing. All of these reasons are valid. The important thing is to know why you are entering into the deal, and to make sure that whomever you deal with is providing you with a valuable service or putting more money in your pocket than you would otherwise earn.[61]

A deal may be for a single song, where a songwriter and publisher agree to enter into a deal covering only one of the songwriter's songs. Another type of deal binds the songwriter as an *exclusive* songwriter for the publishing company for a specific period of time. This means the publishing company will be the publisher of every song the songwriter writes during the term of the agreement. A variation of the exclusive songwriter deal is a writer-artist development deal, where the publisher is actively trying to land a record deal for the songwriter who is also an artist. If the publisher is successful in getting a record deal for the songwriter/artist, presumably many of the songwriter/publisher-owned songs will be on the album.

Often, songwriters receive advances from a full-service publishing company on the anticipated income stream their songs are expected to generate. If the songwriter is an exclusive songwriter for the publishing company, this provides the songwriter with a steady income that frees the songwriter from

---

61 Along the same lines, do not be surprised if an artist who agrees to use your song changes a few of the words and asks to be included as a songwriter on the song. Remember, it is about money. If you need the artist more than the artist needs your song, it may be worth including the artist as one of the songwriters of the song. A co-writer of one song on a Beyoncé album makes much more than a writer of many songs that appear on an album of a lesser-known artist.

monthly economic worry. As part of this type of deal with a full-service publishing company, a new songwriter may be expected to give up all of his or her interest in the publisher's share (i.e., 50% of the gross dollars earned). This, however, may not be necessary if the publisher believes in your songs, and you are willing to take smaller advances against anticipated income from royalties. Advances for new aspiring songwriters, who are not also *artists*, rarely exceed $2,000 per month, and for the most part, are paid only in Nashville. Outside of Nashville, unless the songwriter is already a signed recording artist, is an aspiring artist for whom the major publishing company believes it can land a record deal, or has a unique "in" with a major recording artist, a major publishing company is not likely to offer the songwriter any deal.

There are many nuances that define the various deals a songwriter may enter into with a publisher. Songwriters often enter into what are referred to as *co-publishing* deals and *administrative* deals. These terms mean different things to different people in the industry, and what they mean must be spelled out in each contract.

A *co-publishing* deal is entered into by a songwriter and a publisher when the songwriter and publisher agree to share the publishing. This type of deal is often entered into when the songwriter's songs are expected to generate a lot of income for the publishing company, and the songwriter has his or her own outlets for the songs. Typically, in deals such as these, the publisher's share of income is split 50/50. This means that the songwriter retains 75% of the songs' earning power (i.e., 100% of the songwriter's share and 50% of the publisher's share).

If a straight *administration* deal is entered into by a

songwriter and a publisher, there will be no advances, and the publishing company will limit its role to administrative tasks. Copyright ownership of the songs may be retained by a separate publishing entity controlled by the songwriter, the term of the agreement may be shorter, and a lesser percentage of publishing (i.e., the publisher's share) will be given to the administrative publishing company. Typically, the administrative publisher receives 7.5% to 20% of the gross dollars earned in such deals. The more income a songwriter's songs have generated in previous years, the lower the publisher's percentage. Also, the specific services rendered play a part in determining the percentage earned by the publishing company. For instance, a publishing company that specializes in administrative deals, but also helps songwriters find users for their songs — a function considered *creative* — may charge more for the added service provided.

15. KEY PUBLISHING CONTRACT DEAL POINTS

As with the key record contract deal points (Chapter 8), the key points discussed below, to one extent or another, deal with where money ends up — in the songwriter's pocket or in the publisher's pocket. (A songwriter may own a part of the publisher's share, but will own the entire songwriter's share.)

Keep this list as a handy reference tool when you are negotiating, or renegotiating, your publishing deal. Insist that your lawyer explain each item to you in detail.

1) TERM

The term of an exclusive songwriter deal with a major publisher will usually be tied to the delivery of a minimum number of songs, or will be for one year, with the publisher granted the right to exercise several consecutive one-year options. Try to limit the number of options to three or fewer. A writer-artist development deal may be for as long as two years. This allows the publisher more time to get the songwriter a record deal. If it is successful, the publishing house will generally insist on having an option to extend the publishing agreement for the life of the record deal.

2) RIGHTS TRANSFERRED / USE OF SONG(S)

The publisher will want transferred to it all of the songwriter's rights. Yet, there are some rights you may not wish your publisher to exercise. You may wish to limit your publisher's right to do one or more of the following without your approval:

a.   Change the title of the song.

b.   Change the words or music.

c.   Allow it to be synchronized to X-rated films.

d.   Allow it to be synchronized to advertisements.

e.   Translate the words into a foreign language.

f.   Allow someone else to modify your song and share in the royalties from the derivative work.

Also, remember that *compulsory* mechanical licenses to others need not be issued until the song has first been recorded and distributed publicly in phonorecords with the copyright owner's permission. A songwriter who is also an artist may want to deny the publisher the right to issue a negotiated license to anyone other than the songwriter until after the songwriter's song has appeared on his or her own album.

Finally, the publisher may ask the songwriter to transfer all rights to all of the songwriter's material written prior to the date the agreement was entered into. If this is the case, make sure that you are being compensated for these additional songs.

3) ROYALTIES

Major publishing companies are often owned by a parent company that owns a major record and/or film company. Make sure the publisher cannot issue mechanical licenses at less than customary rates to its affiliated companies. Do this even if you are entitled to receive part of the publisher's share of income.

Your contract with the publisher should call for "the songwriter" to receive 50% of *all* monies collected (except performing rights monies paid directly to the songwriter from a performing rights society such as ASCAP or BMI).

4) ADVANCES

If a songwriter signs an agreement with a major publishing company allowing his or her songs to be published by the publishing company, the publishing company may agree to pay the songwriter advances on its anticipated profits from the songwriter's songs. The larger the percentage of profits given up by the songwriter, the higher the advance should be. The amount of the advance is based on how much money the publishing company expects to make from the songs. The range is from $0 to a high percentage of the money earned by the songwriter's songs in the previous year(s). When a new *artist*, who happens also to be a songwriter, is signed by a major label record company, publishing companies will offer him or her an advance in exchange for a portion of his or her publishing. This amount can be well over $100,000 if the publisher believes the record company will strongly push the artist/songwriter's record, or if a bidding war breaks out. Of course, the advances will be recoupable from royalties and fees when actually received by the publishing company from licensees.

Often, the publisher negotiates to receive advances from third parties to whom they license the songs. For instance, a record company may give the publishing company an advance against anticipated mechanical royalties the publishing company and songwriter will earn from a record that is going to be released. The agreement between the songwriter and publisher should include a provision entitling the songwriter to participate in all advances paid to the publisher by third parties for licenses.

5) RESERVE LIMITATIONS

Usually, publishers are paid by record companies quarterly,

and reserves of 30% to 40% are retained by the record company. These reserves are often held for as long as two years. Since record companies do not have cross-collateralization rights against publishers, the way they do against artists, most record companies are extremely wary when it comes time to release the reserve to the publishing house. In any event, just because you have a song on a major album, don't expect to see any money immediately.

Even though record companies pay the publisher quarterly, publishers typically try to pay the songwriter only twice a year. Every effort should be made to get your publisher to pay you quarterly.

6) COPYRIGHT OWNERSHIP REVERSION

Generally, the rights to your song(s) are sold to the publisher for the life of the copyright in exchange for your participation in royalty and other payments.[62] You should try to negotiate for reversion of the copyright if certain criteria are not met by the publisher (e.g., placing a song on a record within a certain time period, earning a pre-set amount on your song(s)).

7) WORK FOR HIRE

Remember, the copyright of a work for hire is owned from the outset by the person or entity doing the hiring, not the

---

[62] If the original owner of a copyrighted work created after January 1, 1978 sends timely notice to the publisher, the United States publishing rights revert back to the original owner after 35 years. Note that the reversion is for U.S rights only, not international rights. (The notice can be sent as early as 10 years before the effective date of the reversion.) The additional 39 years for older copyrighted works also revert back to the original copyright owner upon giving effective notice.

actual songwriter. Make sure that your publishing contract specifically states that your songs are not works for hire and are not written within the scope of employment by the publisher. Even if a publisher offers to pay you your share of royalties in exchange for making your songs works for hire, it is not in your best interest to do so. If one of your songs becomes a standard, it will have value for many years. One of the quirks in the U.S. copyright law allows the original owner of a song to reclaim full copyright ownership after 35 years.[63] If you are not the original owner, you will not be entitled to exercise this right of copyright reversion.[64]

8) MINIMUM SONG DELIVERY

In most publishing contracts, especially those in which a publishing company is paying the songwriter an advance, a minimum song delivery requirement is added to ensure that the songwriter is actually working. Typically, this averages about twelve songs per year (one per month). If you deliver a song co-written with someone else (i.e., you collaborate 50/50 with another writer), you will receive credit for having delivered half of one song to the publisher. You'll need to deliver 11.5 more.

9) COLLABORATIONS

Make sure there are no prohibitions against collaborating with songwriters who have other publishers. You should only be responsible for transferring your share of ownership of the collaborated song to the publisher.

---

[63] See footnote 62.

[64] Never allow your song to be referred to in any contract as a "work for hire," unless you are being paid considerable money for a particular project (e.g., to work on a film).

10) EXCEPTIONS TO EXCLUSIVITY

Even though a songwriter's agreement may be exclusive, there may be certain situations that you wish to exclude from your agreement with the publisher. For instance, if you are writing a song specifically for a film, oftentimes the film company will insist on receiving the copyright and you may need this flexibility.

Also, for contracts with publishers in California, be aware of Civil Code §3423(e) and Code of Civil Procedure §526(5), both of which deal with personal service contracts. Essentially, these code provisions deny a publisher the right to obtain an injunction to stop you from writing songs for someone else (even if you agreed to provide the publisher your exclusive services), unless the publisher pays you a minimum compensation of $9,000 in the first contract year, $12,000 in the second year, $15,000 in the third year, and substantially more in years four through seven.

11) CO-PUBLISHING ISSUES

A co-publishing deal is entered into not only when a songwriter keeps part of his or her publishing, but also if two "real" publishing companies are publishers of a song (e.g., when songwriters collaborating on a song have different publishers).

If there is a co-publishing deal, two major issues arise apart from "official" ownership of the copyright. The first issue is: who does the administration for the song (and gets paid to do so)? It is always better to have you, or your publisher, keep the administration.

The other major issue is determining what monies get divided among the various publishers. This amount can be disputed because each publisher may be performing different functions and incurring different costs in doing so.

12) INFRINGEMENT CLAIMS

We live in a lawsuit-happy society. Anyone can claim that you infringed on their song and start a costly legal battle. A publishing company will generally insist on 1) being indemnified by you for the full costs of the lawsuit; 2) retaining control over the litigation; and 3) holding as a *reserve* (instead of paying you) the money that is being sued for, regardless of whether the lawsuit is justified or not. At the very least, a songwriter should insist that if the lawsuit is unsuccessful, the publisher will pay for its share of the legal fees.

13) LIMITS ON FOREIGN SUB-PUBLISHER FEES

Most publishers use foreign sub-publishers to collect royalties from other countries because of the nuances particular to each country. If the agreement between the songwriter and publisher states that the songwriter and publisher are to split the net foreign royalties received by the publisher (after the sub-publisher takes its fees), then the songwriter, at least to some extent, is really paying for publishing twice. A songwriter should try to receive royalties *at the source*. This means that the songwriter will share royalties 50/50 *before* the sub-publisher's share is deducted.

14) ACCOUNTING AND AUDITING RIGHTS

You should be sure your contract requires a periodic accounting from the publishing company that details: 1) payments received from record companies; 2) other licensing fees received by the publisher for use of your songs; 3) payments from sub-publishers; and 4) expenses charged to your account. Also, insist that the contract allow you to conduct a detailed audit of the publisher's books. The more rights you have, the better. This can help prevent the publishing company from becoming sloppy with your account.

15) PUBLISHING AND 360 RECORD DEALS

For the most part, if you, as a new *artist*, want to sign a record deal, you will be required to give the record company part of the earnings from your publishing. Your lawyer should negotiate to give *passive* rights, meaning that you give the record company a percentage of net income, but you keep the publishing rights. Also, since publishing income comes in a variety of flavors, try to limit the record company's share to mechanical rights, and from your recordings only. Give up more publishing income from more sources only as necessary. And if the record company would like you to sign on with its publishing company affiliate, don't be shy about asking for added advances for sharing the publishing. Additionally, make sure the record company isn't allowed to continue sharing your publishing income if they drop you as an artist.

Finally, as I mentioned in Chapter 6, **never allow the royalty payments due you as an *artist* from your record deal to be cross-collateralized with royalty payments due you as a *songwriter*.**

16. CREATING YOUR OWN PUBLISHING COMPANY

Here is a basic guide to creating your own publishing company. There are three essential steps:

Step 1: If you are a songwriter and are setting up your own publishing company, before you do anything else, first apply for affiliation with a performance rights society. The reason to do this is because if the name of your company is similar to others, ASCAP/BMI will turn the application down (i.e., they will not collect money for you). It is therefore smart to apply before your company has spent money on promotional material. SESAC has a more selective process for affiliation, so I have limited my discussion below to ASCAP and BMI. More information about SESAC can be found at www.sesac.com.

You must apply *separately* as a songwriter and as a publisher to the *same* performance rights society (i.e., apply to either ASCAP as both a songwriter and publisher *or* apply to BMI as both a songwriter and publisher). If your intention is to become a publishing company for other songwriters as well, separate applications as a publisher to both ASCAP and BMI should be made, and two different publishing company names must be chosen and used. It can take over one month to get approved.

ASCAP and BMI will provide you with lists of names currently being used by publishing companies affiliated with them. BMI will even reserve a company name for you (upon request and for a limited time only) if it is not being used by another publisher.

You can contact ASCAP and BMI as follows:

ASCAP:

1900 Broadway, New York, NY 10023;
tel. (212) 621-6000; or

7920 Sunset Blvd, 3rd Floor, Los Angeles, CA 90046;
tel. (323) 883-1000; or

Two Music Square West, Nashville, TN 37203;
tel. (615) 742-5000.

ASCAP's website: www.ascap.com
also, tel. (800) 95ASCAP

BMI:

7 World Trade Center, 250 Greenwich Street,
New York, NY 10019;
tel. (212) 220-3000; or

8730 Sunset Blvd, 3rd Floor,
West Hollywood, CA 90069;
tel. (310) 659-9109; or

10 Music Square East, Nashville, TN 37203;
tel. (615) 401-2000.

BMI's website: www.bmi.com. BMI can
also be reached via e-mail at: losangeles@bmi.com,
nashville@bmi.com and newyork@bmi.com.

ASCAP and BMI also have offices in Atlanta, Miami
London and Puerto Rico.

Step 2: If your company is not a corporation using its corporate name, in most states it must file a document with the county recorder in which the publishing company is located stating, among other things, the business name that you are operating under. The exact name of the document and the specific requirements vary from state to state, but your county recorder should be able to guide you through your state's particular maze.

In California, the document is called the Fictitious Business Name Statement ("FBNS"). The FBNS must not only be filed with the county recorder's office, but must also appear in a newspaper of general circulation. Your county recorder can tell you which newspapers are acceptable and, based on circulation, which is probably the least expensive.

Step 3: Register the songs with the Copyright Office in Washington, D.C., in the name of your publishing entity. If you have previously registered the songs, file an assignment transferring the copyright ownership of the songs to the publishing entity.

♪ ♪ ♪

Well, it's time for a break. The following pages contain THE "BIG PICTURE" ROYALTY CHART that summarizes the largest royalty payments, and other fees paid to artists and songwriters.

THE "BIG PICTURE"

ARTIST'S LARGEST ROYALTIES

Record Royalties:

From record sales. Paid by the record company to the artist in exchange for allowing the record company to make a record featuring the artist.

The amount paid is typically a percentage of the wholesale published price to dealers (PPD) of the record, less many deductions.

Downloads from sites such as iTunes are included as record sales for which an artist gets paid.

Performing Royalties:

From having the recordings played. Paid by radio stations in many foreign countries, digital satellite radio broadcasters (Sirius XM), and certain non-interactive digital music streamers such as Pandora.

Terrestrial am/fm radio stations and TV stations in the United States do not pay performing royalties.

Performing royalties are paid 1) by contract to a record co. (which then pays the artist) or 2) by statute to a non-profit performance rights organization called SoundExchange. If paid to SoundEx. the collected fees are distributes to the record company and the artist directly.

Other Fees & Royalties:

From advertisement, film/TV, ringtones, the internet, having part of the record being sampled, video games and DVD use license fees. Paid by film companies, television production companies, phone companies, internet based companies, interactive digital music streamers such as Rhapsody, video game makers, video streamers, and many others to the record company for the right to use the record company's master recording of the artist's version of the song.

The record company pays the artist his or her share of the fees or royalties as agreed to in the record contract.

ROYALTY CHART

SONGWRITER'S LARGEST ROYALTIES

Mechanical Royalties:

From record sales. Paid by a record company to the publisher for the right to include the songwriter's song on a record. The publisher pays the songwriter his or her share.

The publisher receives 100% of this royalty, which is divided into two equal parts (50/50) called 1) the *writer's share*, and 2) the *publisher's share*.

The publisher pays the songwriter the entire *writer's share*.

The publisher pays the songwriter any part of the *publisher's share* retained by the songwriter in the agreement between the songwriter and publisher.

Performing Royalties:

From airplay, audio streaming, and being played in public. Paid by radio and TV stations, digital music streamers*, live venues, many stores, and other public users of a song.

This royalty is divided into two equal parts (50/50) called 1) the *writer's share*, and 2) the *publisher's share*. Monies are paid to ASCAP/BMI/SESAC.

These "performance rights societies" pay the songwriter directly the entire *writer's share*. The society pays the publisher the *publisher's share*. If part of the *publisher's share* is retained by the songwriter, the publisher pays the songwriter that part of the *publisher's share*.

Other Fees & Royalties:

From advertisement, film/TV, ringtones, the internet, sheet music sales, having part of the song on a record being sampled, video games and DVD use license fees. Paid by film companies, television production companies, phone companies, internet based companies, sheet music companies, and many others to the publisher for the right to use a song.

The publisher receives 100% of fees and royalties from the use of the song and, in turn, pays the songwriter his or her share in the same manner that mechanical royalties are paid to the songwriter.

*Interactive audio streaming earns both a mechanical and performing royalty.

OTHER IMPORTANT BASICS

17. ISSUES BETWEEN BAND MEMBERS

This is one of the least favorite things for band members to discuss. When you are just starting out, everything is great because it's all about the music. The individual members do not have divergent interests. Strong artistic differences haven't surfaced, and there is no money at stake to fight over. Issues between band members, however, must be discussed.

Apart from enjoying the music, make sure that you really like being with the other members of your band. If you are successful, you will be touring together, promoting your band together, and generally spending a great deal of time together.

Not only does spending time with people you don't like become old very quickly, but like it or not, *you will also be in business with them.*

Life is too short for the nightmares that follow when the inevitable disagreements about money surface. If you haven't had success yet, you won't think money is an issue, but it will be. When band members do not like each other, money fights can become very nasty.

When a band is just forming, you cannot anticipate or protect against all of the things that may happen, and until you truly believe that the band is going somewhere, it doesn't make sense to spend a lot of money on a lawyer. But, once you believe the band is going to be together for a while, it makes sense to hire a lawyer and have an internal band contract drawn up, be it in the form of a partnership, a corporation or a limited liability company.

A good contract between band members will address critical issues including the following:

1. Who owns the band's name in the event of a breakup?
2. Who gets what percentages of profits?
3. How are artistic decisions made if there is a disagreement?
4. Who controls the band's business decisions such as when to tour or firing other band members?
5. What happens to a former member's interest if he or she quits or is fired? and,
6. Who owns and controls the band's website and fan database?

If you are the "Pete Best" of the group (the Beatles' drummer before Ringo Starr), waiting until a major-label record deal is at hand to address these questions may be too late. It's better to find out early on where everybody stands.

Another critical question that band members must address is who owns what songwriting and publishing interests. Does each member own the individual copyright to the songs he or she wrote, or does the band own the copyrights to all the band's songs? How about something in the middle (e.g., the person who actually wrote the song owns a bit more of the song)? And, what happens to the copyrights if the band later breaks up?

If, for example, each band member individually owns the copyrights to their respective songs, the band may be in for a fight when the members try to agree on which song is going to become the album's single; the song with all the airplay, featured on iTunes. As you will recall from earlier chapters, a band (as artists) can be losing money even though at the same time, the person writing the songs for the band is making a great deal of money. It is easy for the band to come apart when most of the band is still struggling financially, but the songwriting member is living in a new home in Beverly Hills.

So what happens if the band does not have a written contract? The band is treated as a legal partnership. Each member of the band is presumed to 1) share equally in the band's profits and losses, and 2) have an equal vote in the band's affairs. Majority rules! And like a partnership, when one of the band members (i.e., one of the partners) leaves the band, for whatever reason, then legally that partnership terminates automatically.

Of course, the remaining members of the band are free to form a new band, but legally, they may not be free to use the old band's name without paying the departing member for the privilege of doing so. Payment may be due because without a written contract, the law generally presumes that each original band member owns an equal share of the band's physical assets (e.g., the equipment) *and* intangible assets (e.g., the band's name and logo).

Apart from issues centering around the band's formation and demise, terms of the band's record deal itself may leave a band member's ego bruised. Certain sensitive matters will be spelled out, by necessity, in the record contract. Is the record company going to treat one member as more valuable than the rest? If one member refuses to record, are all the members in breach of the contract? If one member leaves the group, does the record company have the right to void the record deal? Who is responsible to the record company if the band is still "in the red" when one member leaves the band?

A good contract between band members will address the rights and obligations of each individual member. Work out the details with your attorney — including whether or when to set up as a limited liability company or a corporation instead of a partnership — before you get too big, or you may be in for some ugly legal fights down the road.

18. TRADEMARKS & SERVICE MARKS

Your band name and logo as a band are potentially valuable assets. You can cripple your future earning power before your career even begins if you don't have an identity that is your own and can't be used by others.

Often, people use the term *copyright* when they really mean *trademark* or *service mark*. Basically, the difference is that copyrights protect the expression of artistic ideas — for example, a songwriter's songs — and trademarks/service marks protect the identifying symbols associated with a particular product or service (e.g., a brand name or a logo).[65]

More specifically, a *trademark* is a word, phrase, symbol or design[66] which identifies you as the *source of goods* and distinguishes you from others offering similar goods. A *service mark* is the same thing except that it identifies and distinguishes you as the *source of a service*.

Your band's name is used to identify services offered — i.e., the performance of your music — and therefore is considered a service mark.[67]

---

[65] Copyrights are discussed more fully in Chapter 10.

[66] Or a combination of words, phrases, symbols and design. Sounds and colors can also qualify as marks.

[67] Note, however, that when you are offering merchandise for sale with the band's name on it (e.g., T-shirts or caps), the same mark (i.e., your band's name) can be used as a trademark.

In the United States, when two bands are fighting over a band name that does not infringe on anyone else's service mark or trademark, the right to use the particular band name generally belongs to the band that first uses the name in commerce.[68] A service mark is considered used when the service mark is included in advertising or other promotional material and the service is actually being provided (e.g., your band is a real playing band). Incidentally, the name is not owned by the person in the band who thought it up, but rather by who uses the name (i.e., the band). If a particular member of the band wants to own the band's name, this can be set up through an internal band contract.

Watch out for managers who attempt to control the band's name. I know of a popular band from the sixties and seventies that still occasionally tours underground because the members fear the legal wrath of their former manager who owns the right to use the name. Years ago, members of Justin Timberlake's boy band, ★NSYNC, had to settle a huge lawsuit with the manager who started their career so they could keep using the name. Of course, the members have gone their separate ways for now. But that could change in a heartbeat when the timing is right.

Before picking a band name that you are truly attached

---

[68] There are two main exceptions to this: 1) before you actually began to use the mark, another band filed an application with the U.S. Patent and Trademark Office stating that they intend to use the mark, and the other band's mark later matures to registration; or 2) another band files an application for a mark with the U.S. Patent and Trademark Office which is based on a valid foreign mark that it filed before you began using the mark, *and* the other band filed with the U.S. Patent and Trademark Office within six months of the filing of the original foreign application. The foreign band's mark will have priority over yours if its mark matures to registration.

to and want to keep throughout your career, here are two important suggestions:

1. **Do a search of potentially conflicting marks.** When you make it big, you don't want another band suing you because it was using the name before you were. Even if the other band's name is not actually the same as yours, you could still find yourself prevented from using your chosen name.

The key legal test of whether a band name infringes on someone else's service mark or trademark is the "*likelihood of confusion*" but as with a growing number of legal issues today, there is no specific definition of what constitutes a likelihood of confusion. Rather, there are a number of factors that come into play and are used by courts to determine the actual likelihood of confusion. Factors include the similarity in the overall impression created by the two marks, the similarities of the goods and services involved, and evidence of actual confusion by consumers.

The best way to make sure that your name will be afforded mark protection — even though no method is foolproof — is to hire a professional search company to search the records of the U.S. Patent and Trademark Office ("PTO"), the trademark records of all fifty states, and to also locate unregistered marks. This will cost several hundred dollars. Two well-respected firms are CT Corsearch; tel. (800) 732-7241; www.corsearch.com, and Thomson Compumark; tel. (800) 692-8833; www.trademarks. thomsonreuters.com.

If you cannot afford to hire a professional search firm, at least make an effort to check trade sources such as: 1) the AFM (American Federation of Musicians) — whose offices will tell you whether the AFM has an exclusive agency contract with a group already using the name you want; tel. (212) 869-1330 in New York, or (323) 461-5401 in California; www. afm.org; 2) *Billboard's International Talent & Touring Directory* — this directory lists most of the groups actively performing; and 3) the websites of ASCAP, BMI and SESAC. Also, for federally registered marks only, and *not* for marks registered with a particular state, the PTO also has a search mechanism on its website. The PTO website is www.uspto.gov. You can also search the internet to see if the name you want to use is being used by someone else — a Google search, a domain name search, a Twitter search, a Facebook search, an iTunes search... you get the idea.

2. **Make the name of your band distinctive.** After you have been using your mark, the distinctiveness of it will increase your ability to prevent others from using a mark that may create confusion with your mark.[69]

♪ ♪ ♪

Even though trademark and service mark rights are generally created by use, and not by registration with either the PTO or an individual state's Secretary of State, it is a good idea when you start becoming successful to register the name of

---

[69] Theoretically, a service mark or trademark cannot be registered if it consists of "immoral matter."

[70] Of course, it is more prudent to register your mark before you begin using it, but, as I will discuss shortly, it can be quite costly to do so. If you see the symbol ® at the end of a mark, it means that the mark has been federally registered with the PTO. Incidentally, the symbols TM and SM that you have probably come across are unofficial and are used only to give notice to others that you claim trademark (TM) or service mark (SM) ownership in an unregistered mark. You can use these liberally if you wish. Because people are afraid that it will make their 'art' seem commercial, TM and SM do not seem to be used often in the entertainment industry.

your band with the PTO.[70] To do so, you must first engage in, or anticipate engaging in, interstate commerce (e.g., playing in another state, selling CDs in another state, or offering for sale a CD via an internet site with reach beyond your home state). By registering your mark, if another band infringes on it by using a conflicting mark, you will have access to the courts and will be able to obtain an injunction to stop the other band cold.[71]

You can reach the PTO at www.uspto.gov or as follows: United States Patent and Trademark Office, P.O. Box 1450, Alexandria, VA 22313-1450; tel. (800) 786-9199. When you file an application to register a mark, the PTO first looks for other marks that may be the same as, or similar to, yours. If the application doesn't appear to be in conflict with other marks, the PTO published your proposed mark in the *Official Gazette of the United States Patent and Trademark Office* so that others can look at your mark and raise objections, if they have any. It usually takes over a year to obtain the registration even if everything goes perfectly and no one has any objection to the registration of your mark.

Proper registration of a mark can cost thousands of dollars. This is because the PTO classifies different goods and services in forty-five separate *classes,* and a separate fee is charged to register a mark in each class. For example, to register your band's name as performers of music (class 41) is different from registering your band's name for use on T-shirts (class 25). In addition, fees paid to the PTO do not include your attorneys' fees, which will be a minimum of several hundred dollars, assuming everything goes smoothly.

---

[71] Note however, that at present, your band is not afforded any service mark or trademark protection from merely obtaining its own internet domain name. You must also show an actual use in commerce.

I strongly suggest that you do not attempt to register your mark without enlisting the help of an attorney who specializes in trademark/service mark law. The importance of properly protecting your mark is great, and there are simply too many ways to leave yourself exposed.

19. ON TOUR

Touring occurs year round, but the major touring season occurs during the summer months. No one except major stars makes big money touring. But as record sales decline, live performance is becoming increasingly important to the industry.

The contracts used for tours booked by music agents are customarily AFM standard printed forms. The real guts of such tour agreements, however, are attached to the form. The attachment is called a *rider* to the contract, and it can be over twenty-five pages long. Important items of negotiation include merchandising rights, limiting promoter expenses, and technical specifications such as an artist's equipment, lighting and stage setup requirements.

If, for any reason, you (as an artist or a band) are booking your own tours, always make sure you have a written contract signed by the club owner *before* you show up to perform at a club. Many times, the dates of performance, compensation, and the sound equipment to be provided get screwed up if an artist does not have a written contract.

New artists should not tour until their record is out. If you recently uploaded a few songs to YouTube or just made your first CD and are getting only a little play online or on college radio, don't expect any club to pay you more than a few hundred dollars a night. More than likely, the club will give you a percentage of the gross proceeds from ticket sales. The percentage may be as high as 65% or so, but may be a lot lower if other artists are playing there that night as well.

If an artist's record is beginning to sell well, the artist can get paid $1,000 to $15,000 a night for headlining at a large club, and up to $15,000 or $20,000 for opening for a major act at an amphitheater or stadium. This may sound like pretty good money, but in many cases the artist will agree to a significantly reduced payment, especially if he or she wants exposure to the headliner's audience. And oftentimes, when headlining at a club, the contract still calls for the artist to receive a percentage of the gross proceeds from ticket sales. In the final analysis, an artist must compare the gross income received to the actual expense of going on tour.

It can *easily* cost $10,000 or more to economically put a band on the road for a week without the members drawing any salary — you must pay for food and lodging, equipment rental, truck or bus rental, a minimal crew, insurance, and commissions to agents and managers. And in 360 deals with record companies, 20% to 30% of tour profits go to the record company. An artist or a band can lose a lot of money by going on tour! Sometimes, money may be advanced by the record company as tour support because the record company expects part of the profits, and also wants the artist out there selling records.

A moderately successful artist may be able to make money on tours, but they can actually lose money as well. The key is controlling expenses. He or she may headline in 2000-seat venues and take in $10,000 or more per night, but, unless the artist's fans are willing to pay north of $25 for the show, the show could be a money loser. For the most part, unless you are a major star, or have a low budget act, the primary business purpose of a tour is still to sell records (and other merchandise), and to build brand.

Major stars do make money on tours even though the

costs can be astronomical. Ticket prices have gone through the roof, and major stars also receive money from tour sponsors like Budweiser or Apple.

As for costs, major stars with larger-than-life shows may take 10 luxury buses and many more huge trucks just to put their act on the road — and there may be a chartered jet as well. U2's *360° Tour*, the highest grossing concert tour of all time, cost a small fortune to put on. When you add all the costs, including a touring production crew of over 100 people, and a local crew of over 100 people as well, *daily* productions costs were approximately $750,000.

Major stars get paid minimum guarantees (up to several hundred thousand dollars per night) *or* a percentage of net profits of the show (85%-90% is typical) whichever is larger. The promoter keeps the rest. Because promoters have all sorts of funny ways to add expenses to a concert, thereby reducing "net" profits that must be shared with an artist, some superstar artists now insist on getting paid a percentage of the promoters gross income (usually 65%-70%).[72]

Because major stars make more money from touring, and less from record sales,[73] a bit of power has shifted in the industry from record companies to the people controlling the venues and the ticket sales.

---

[72] The split is not based on *total* concert gross income. It is based on *net gross* to the promoter. The *net gross* concept allows the promoter to deduct certain items from the total gross receipts that don't flow to the promoter. For example, a ticket price surcharge added by the venue is excluded from the *net gross*.

[73] Amazingly, at least to me anyway, more than 50% of the top 100 grossing acts contain artists over 60 years old. Their best record selling days may be over, but their fans still love them.

Like the rest of the maturing music business, there has been consolidation in ownership and control of the top touring venues. Currently, one company, Live Nation Entertainment, owns or operates over 80% of the large amphitheaters in the U.S. This company also owns Ticketmaster.

Control of venues and concert dates, not only the deal money involved, may have prompted Madonna and Jay-Z to sign mega 360 deals with Live Nation, rather than with traditional record companies — though agreements were reached with traditional record companies to handle record distribution. Madonna's record sales may have waned (relative to previous Madonna releases), but her 2012 *MDNA* tour was the top grossing tour of the year. As for Jay-Z, in 2013 he struck a new deal with Universal Music Group to house his music label, Roc Nation. In his own words, he recognized "the strength, power and reach" of Universal. Live Nation does many things well, but it seems no one can sell records like the majors.

20. SELLING MERCHANDISE

Once you have your record deal and publishing deal in place, you will have plenty of advisors to protect you with regard to merchandising. If you have a 360 deal with a record company, the record company will take 20% to 30% of your profits from your merchandising deal.

If you are just starting out, you are probably selling your own CDs, silk-screened T-shirts and caps at your shows. I do not mean to scare you (and as long as you are relatively small no one may care very much), but be aware that when you sell merchandise, there are rules. There are city taxes, state taxes, business license fees and other local fees that must be paid. If you have a "roadie" or a friend doing the selling for you, either may technically be an employee of yours, and payroll taxes must be paid. In any event, you probably won't be making a lot of money from merchandise sales until you hit the big time.

With rare exceptions, during a tour of a successful artist, the artist will license the right to use his or her name and likeness to a merchandiser. Two of the larger tour merchandisers are Bravado International Group and Live Nation Merchandising. In the U.S., the royalty paid to the artist is generally 30% to 40% of the gross sales of the merchandise. Major stars, of course, can receive more than 40% of the gross.

Merchandise can fly off the shelves during a concert. After spending a great deal of money on the concert itself, fans want a memory of the event and the artist. Special T-shirts alone can fetch $40 or more. Some people literally spend hundreds of dollars on souvenirs. Adult-oriented groups — like the Rolling Stones or Sting — make out pretty well. Heavy metal groups make out even better. And hot touring acts such as Justin Bieber or Taylor Swift, who cater to a younger fan base, make out the best of all.

Keep your image in mind. You don't want schlock out there with your name on it. Items of negotiation with a merchandising company include: the amount of advances to the artist, creative control over the merchandise, the merchandiser's exclusive right to market, performance guarantees (that the artist or band will show up and play before a given number of people during the tour), and sell-off rights of excess merchandise at the end of the tour.

For merchandise sold at places other than concerts, the royalties paid by merchandisers to the artist for the right to manufacture the goods — or sub-license someone else to do so in the U.S.— are generally a lot less. One night of sales at a major concert can net the artist more than a full year of nationwide retail sales. Typically, royalties for clothing — mostly T-shirts and caps — sold at traditional retail outlets and online stores are 15% to 25% of the wholesale sales price, but for sales at mass merchants such as Wal-Mart and Target your royalty payment will be reduced by 50%.

One note of caution if you are a new artist searching the internet for a company to print your T-shirts: don't enter into any agreement with any company that gives the company an exclusive right to use your name, likeness or logo. If you end up as famous as The Rolling Stones, you will want the rights to profit from your version of the Stones' tongue.

21. A LITTLE ABOUT MUSIC VIDEOS

Thirty years ago, the trade magazine *Billboard* estimated that consistent exposure on MTV was boosting record sales by 15% to 20%. This started a boom. Fast-forward to the year 2000, and music videos were on television everywhere. But in the second decade of the 21st century, MTV doesn't even have a program dedicated to music videos anymore. Music videos receive their major exposure on YouTube and other social media internet sites. Super slick, cutting-edge, big-budget professional videos are thought to be less important than they once were in boosting record sales. Some money can be earned back from the shared ad revenue generated from video streaming.

The typical cost of making a professional video is $15,000 to $50,000. But for a major star, the production value can lead costs to rise to $250,000 or even higher. You can, however, make a decent video for under $10,000 and upload it to various websites or have it played on local television. Even at this reduced cost, however, it still may not be a good use of your funds, when you compare it to other methods of promotion. If you feel you must make a video, — YouTube, Facebook, MySpace homemade uploads aside — here are a few budget saving tips that have been passed on to me from people familiar with production:

1. Use exterior daylight or minimal lighting.
2. Forget dance numbers.
3. Put your money into editing the video and syncing the music to it; rely on favors for rehearsal space, for getting the best video and sound equipment you can, and for the video shoot itself.

MUSIC, MOTION PICTURES, TELEVISION & MULTIMEDIA

This topic really requires a book of its own. It will probably not be too important to an artist or songwriter who is not already signed to a record or publishing deal — or is not a good friend of one of the following: a movie/television music coordinator, a video game or DVD producer, an executive with an advertising music supplier, or a big shot with an online or app development company in need of music. Nevertheless, the following pages contain some highlights.

Remember, there is no compulsory license that allows film companies, television production companies, video game makers, DVD producers, advertising agencies, app developers, video streamers, or podcasters to use your song or your performance of a song without permission. Therefore, the fees are negotiable and can vary greatly.

22. THEATRICAL MOTION PICTURES

To obtain the rights to use even one performance of a song as part of a motion picture, a film company may need to enter into many separate contracts. The film company may need to make deals with the performing artist, the songwriter (and publisher), the record company of the performer (both to use existing masters and clearing the right to use the record company's exclusive artist on the film soundtrack album), and finally, with the record company that is going to make the film soundtrack album.[74]

There are essentially three categories of music that may be part of a motion picture: 1) songs specifically written to be an integral part of a motion picture (e.g., "My Heart Will Go On" in the movie *Titanic*); 2) songs not originally written for the film but used in the film (e.g., Elvis' "Hound Dog" in the movie *Forrest Gump*; and 3) the background music you hear throughout a film while actors are conversing and action is taking place (this is the movie's *score*, also known as the *underscore*).

1) SONGS SPECIFICALLY WRITTEN FOR A PARTICULAR MOTION PICTURE

Before the artist or songwriter can make a deal with the film company, both must make sure they are allowed to do

---

[74] And, heaven forbid, the master recording contains samples from another record. If so, rights need to be negotiated with owners of the sampled recording and song as well.

so under the terms of their record contract and publishing contract, respectively.[75]

The Artist

For a song specifically written for a particular motion picture, the artist receives a flat fee (for the performance itself) and royalties (if a movie soundtrack album is made).[76] The amount of the fee can be all over the board. An established hot artist may receive several hundred thousand dollars. By contrast, a falling star in need of publicity may perform a song for as little as minimum union scale if the film is right. The total royalty paid on the soundtrack album is usually 12% to 14% (divided among all the artists appearing on the album — a typical deal calls for an artist to receive a royalty of 1%-1.3% for each song performed). The royalty percentage can, of course, be higher if one of the artists is a major star. Also of note, an artist's record company will want a portion of the fees paid to the artist and also insist on keeping 50% of the artist's royalties if the soundtrack album is released by another record company (for letting the artist out of its "exclusive" arrangement).

The Songwriter

Typically, a songwriter is hired to write a song for a movie as a *work for hire*. The songwriter's payment is a flat fee plus songwriter royalties. The fee can be anywhere from $0 to $100,000

---

[75] Major artists who write their own songs often negotiate package deals with film and television production companies, whereby the artist/songwriter receives one up-front fee and a combination of royalties that, in effect, merges the royalties earned from being both the artist and the songwriter.

[76] Royalty payments may also be earned from foreign distribution of the film.

or more, depending on how established the songwriter is, and how important the film company believes the song will be to the movie. However, by negotiating what are called *kill fees* into the contract, film companies almost never obligate themselves to use a particular song. With an established songwriter, they will usually agree to pay 50% of the original fee if the song is not used. Film companies also enter into *step deals* — where a film company pays the songwriter a small amount initially to make a demo, and then more later if the film company ultimately decides to use the song. Often, intermediate payments between the initial demo and ultimate completion of a song (i.e., "step" payments) are tied to refinements of the song made by the songwriter at the film company's request.

Even in the typical movie deal — where the song is written as a work for hire — the royalties earned by the songwriter will be the same as if the song was written under an ordinary songwriter deal.[77] Also, if the songwriter is well-established, the songwriter may retain a portion of the *publisher's share* of the song. The reason film companies usually insist on hiring the songwriter on a work for hire basis is so that the songwriter will not be legally able to reclaim full copyright ownership after 35 years.[78]

2) SONGS NOT ORIGINALLY WRITTEN FOR A FILM BUT LATER USED IN A FILM

For songs not originally written for a particular film, but later used in that film, the film company has to acquire a license

---

[77] See Chapter 12, "Primary Sources of Income," Chapter 13, "Secondary Sources of Income," and Chapter 14, "Music Publishing."

[78] See footnote 62.

from the songwriter's publisher, and may also require a license from the artist's record company. Here is how the artist and songwriter get paid:

The Artist

If the film company wants to use a particular version of a song already on a record, the film company must obtain a ***master recording license*** from the record company. This gives the film company the right to use the record company's master recording in its movie. The artist typically receives 50% of the *net* money received by the record company for granting the license (which is typically only 37.5% to 42.5% of the money the record company actually receives). The license fees charged by record companies can range from $5,000 to $250,000. If the deal calls for granting the film company rights to make a soundtrack album, the film company will pay an additional royalty of 11% to 14%. Typically, the artist's record company will retain half of these royalties (for agreeing to let the artist out of the record company's exclusive arrangement) and the artist will receive the other half. But if the film company contracts with the artist's record company to make the soundtrack album, the artist can negotiate to receive the full royalty, not just half.

The Songwriter

In many films, a new recording of a popular song is made by an artist, thereby avoiding any requirement to obtain a master recording license from a particular record company. An established hot artist may receive several hundred thousand dollars to record the song. But whether or not the film company wishes to use a record company's master recording, the film company must still negotiate with the copyright owner of the song (i.e., the publisher) to obtain a *sync license,* giving the film company the right to use the musical composition. Without the sync license, *no* version of the song can be used. Synchronization fees paid to a publisher are often about the same as the fees paid to the record company for use of the master recording ($5,000 to $250,000).

3) THE BACKGROUND SCORE

For writing the score of a major film, the composer will receive a fee ranging from $50,000 to $700,000 — unless you are John Williams or James Horner, in which case the fee is likely to be well over $1,000,000. For lower budget films, the composer may receive only a set recording fund of $125,000 to $175,000. From this amount, after expenses, the composer may end up earning $25,000 or less. In addition to songwriter royalties, the composer, like any artist, may also receive a royalty payment for each record sold (6% to 10%). And, if the composer acts as the producer of the recordings, he or she will receive an additional producer's royalty (3% to 4%).

♪ ♪ ♪

With the necessary use licenses in hand, the film company is free to strike a deal with any record/distribution company to put out a soundtrack album. Often, all three categories of music discussed above are a part of the same film and will be included in varying degrees on the soundtrack album. If only some of the music on a soundtrack album is expected to be the catalyst that generates sales, the amount of royalties different people and entities ultimately receive from the soundtrack album will be heavily contested.

23. TELEVISION

The licenses that must be obtained to use a song on television shows and made-for-TV movies are the same as those for theatrical motion pictures. There are some differences between the two mediums, however. First, unlike songs used in theatrical motion pictures shown in U.S. theaters, the songwriter will receive performing royalties (i.e., ASCAP/BMI/SESAC payments) from songs used on television. Second, in part because payments are received from ASCAP/BMI/SESAC, and in part because the exposure from television is much greater than the exposure from film, payments to the artist and songwriter for songs used in television are much smaller. The TV exposure helps trigger an increase in the other sources of income from a song.

As with theatrical motion pictures, there are essentially three categories of music that may become part of a television program: 1) songs specifically written for a particular television program; 2) songs not originally written for a particular program, but later used in one; and 3) the television background score.

1) SONGS WRITTEN SPECIFICALLY FOR A PARTICULAR TELEVISION PROGRAM

There are not many songs written specifically for a particular television program other than the theme song. Since some television theme songs are composed by the show's background composers, these songs are often included as part of the initial background composing contract (but for an additional fee). This contract will generally state that all the songs written by the composer for the television program are works for hire.

2) SONGS NOT ORIGINALLY WRITTEN FOR A PARTICULAR TELEVISION PROGRAM BUT LATER USED IN ONE

To use a pre-existing song in a television show, the producer must secure the rights to use the song from the publisher. The usual sync licensing fees charged by publishers to use a song in a television program or series for worldwide perpetual distribution range from $1,500 to $3,500. For network television shows, the sync fee can range from $10,000-$20,000, especially if rights to rebroadcast the show in all media are obtained. If a well-known song is going to be used as the theme song for a television program, the publisher may charge the television production company more than $10,000 per episode.

In addition to the sync license from the songwriter's publisher, if the producer wishes to use a particular version of the song that's on a record, a separate master recording license must be obtained from the record company. TV show exposure is like free advertising that promotes future sales of the record company's record, so the fees charged are low, but again, for network shows, the range can be between $10,000-$20,000.

3) THE BACKGROUND SCORE

The background score constitutes the vast majority of music heard on television. Creative fees can range from $3,500 to $20,000 per episode ($10,000 to $30,000 for a package of multiple episodes), depending on such factors as how established the composer is, the length of the program being written for, how much music is needed on the show, and the size of the music budget. As with other music composed for movies and television, the standard television background composing contract states that the composer's music is a work for hire. Therefore, the composer does not retain ownership of the copyright. The composer may, however, retain an interest in the royalties earned by the background score.

♪ ♪ ♪

In a properly negotiated contract, when an American television program or made-for-TV movie is re-released in foreign movie theaters, or on pay television in the U.S., an additional fee will be paid to the artist and/or songwriter (unless all rights have already been granted in exchange for a larger fee). Also, an additional fee is paid if the TV program or movie is distributed for home video use.

24. COMMERCIAL ADVERTISING

Advertisers want their products remembered. One way to do that is through the use of a catchy phrase, matched by a simple catchy tune — a jingle. Jingles are primarily used in advertising on television, radio and online. In order to get your song used as a jingle, you will have to have an "in" with an advertising agency, an advertising music supplier (e.g., a "jingle house" representing many composers), or a producer producing such music. There are essentially two types of songs used as jingles: 1) songs written for a specific advertising campaign, and 2) existing songs.

1) SONGS WRITTEN FOR A SPECIFIC AD CAMPAIGN

After an advertising campaign is selected by a company and its ad agency, a music supplier is hired to provide the music if the agency does not write the music in-house. The music supplier may be an independent writer or a jingle production company that is typically owned by a writer. The ad agency customarily provides the lyrics for the jingle. The amount charged by the music supplier is two-fold: 1) a creative fee (typically ranging from $5,000 to over $50,000 for one 30-second commercial)[79]; and 2) production costs (to cover the costs of hiring musicians and studio rental).

The music supplier provides the finished master and often writes the music as well. As the musician, the music supplier is entitled to residual royalty payments per AFM,

---

[79] If the advertising campaign involves a major celebrity artist/songwriter, the creative fees may exceed one million dollars.

SAG or AFTRA union contracts. In addition, music suppliers, as composers and publishers, may receive a small amount of performing royalties from ASCAP/BMI/SESAC.[80]

2) EXISTING SONGS

If an ad agency wishes to use a particular version of a song already on a record, the agency must obtain a sync license from the songwriter's publisher, *and* a separate master use license from the record company.[81] Avoiding the added cost of getting a master use license is the reason you hear unfamiliar versions of songs in commercials. License fees vary greatly, depending on such factors as whether the song is to be played on TV, radio or the web, the length of the song's use, the song's popularity, the type of product being marketed, and the scope of the ad campaign. For a national commercial, the going rate an advertiser must pay to obtain a master use license and sync license of a popular song ranges from $50,000 to well over $1,000,000. For now, the era of the multi-million dollar sync license payday — as when both Microsoft and Ford paid to be associated with the Rolling Stones' "Start Me Up" — appears to be over.

Yet as musicians recognize the power of co-branding, the artist/songwriter may forego *any* licensing fee at all, depending on the advertiser, and the perceived benefits to an upcoming tour, album, or career. For instance, U2 took no fee for its 2004 breakthrough Apple iPod ad. Nevertheless, financially,

---

[80] If an ad agency wishes to save money, e.g., for a low-budget ad campaign, they may license existing stock music (usually background scores) from a music library or a post-production house. The license fees for such music are generally very low (e.g., less than $100), with no residuals payable to the songwriters. Such music is usually recorded in nonunion sessions abroad.

[81] The ad agency need not obtain a master use license if it re-records a new version of the song; rather, only a sync license is necessary.

U2 benefited greatly from this association with Apple. On the other hand Samsung paid Jay-Z $5 million to allow one million Galaxy phone users to download for free his acclaimed 2013 album *Magna Carta Holy Grail*. This deal worked for both parties. Jay-Z was paid handsomely, and Samsung got bragging rights that it is cooler than Apple.

25. OTHER MULTIMEDIA PLATFORMS & SOURCES OF INCOME

As in motion pictures, television, and pre-existing master recordings used in commercial advertising, if a company wants to include a performance of a song on its exercise DVD or video game, they may need to make separate deals with the performing artist, the songwriter (through the publisher), and the record company of the performer (to use existing masters, and to obtain the right to use the record company's exclusive artist). As with film, TV and existing versions of songs that appear on a record, the artist will receive payment (through his or her record company) for use of the master recording, and the songwriter will receive payment (through his or her publisher) for use of the song.

The types of deals being made, and the dollar amounts involved, are all over the board. Some deals do generate a flat fee of tens of thousands of dollars, while others generate a set number of pennies per each unit sold. Some deals have in-kind promotion or marketing tie-ins as part of the deal (for example, when the company advertises its video game, it has to mention the artist's name — with the artist retaining the right to approve the way his or her name is used, of course).

Here are some of the factors that lead to a higher or lower price: 1) the anticipated unit sales of the specific video game or DVD; 2) the amount of the song or record used; 3) the commercial appeal of the artist; 4) the popularity of the song or record; and 5) the perceived importance of the song or record to the success of the multimedia product.

To use in a video game a particular version of a song already on a record, the video game maker typically pays both the publisher and the record company a licensing fee ranging from $1,500 to $10,000, but the fee can be higher. If an existing record version of a song is used in a music-centered game, such as Guitar Hero, the game maker will pay an advance to the publisher and the record company against a royalty earned for each copy of the game sold, and each download of the song.

Turning to the internet, appreciate that copyright laws are in need of update and clarification as technology continues to race ahead of current laws. Business models also remain unsettled as companies learn how to maximize profits from the use of the internet and digital transmission technology. Although royalty rates for permanent music downloads, non-interactive webcasting, and interactive audio streaming are jelling, royalty rates for apps have not. It can be extremely difficult to determine the appropriate fee that should be paid for using a particular song or performance in some multimedia contexts.[82]

The internet is fragmented. Clearly, the appropriate fee that can be charged to a small business wanting to use a musical clip, or someone wanting to use his or her favorite song on a personal web page, is much different from the fee that can be charged to the company hosting a website with millions of visitors daily. The business model for "fair" pricing doesn't yet exist.

---

[82] Note that I'm not talking about sales of CDs via the internet or downloads of music to smartphones and the like. The royalty rates from these sales are set in your record contract or your publishing deal. The fact that a record is sold via the internet rather than through a traditional retailer doesn't affect your royalty rate unless your record or publishing deal says it does.

So, as an artist, strive to make sure your record deal calls for you to receive your full royalty from all new sources of income flowing to the record company. By all new sources, I mean all future platforms *and* any yet-to-be-invented physical and non-physical formats on which music may be played or heard.

As a songwriter, make sure that your publishing deal calls for you to receive the full songwriter's share of income generated from all sources and all platforms on which music can possibly be played or heard (even if you also own part of the publishing).

And every record and publishing deal must also account for the next wave of cloud computing. The day is likely coming when DVDs and other physical storage of data (for games, educational videos, entertainment videos, or you name it) gives way to always on demand wireless availability of your "stuff," routed to any device you want.

Music used in multimedia platforms ought to be paid for, whether the multimedia product is bought, rented, or just used. Whether it is a new revolutionary game console, a vastly improved smartphone, or some other transformative device, there will be a tendency of some in the music industry to use "new technology" as a justification to lower the payout to artists and songwriters. You and your lawyer must be on guard.

CONCLUSION

Congratulations! You've made it through a lot of difficult information about the deal points and numbers that guide the music business. If I've done my job, you now have a better understanding of the music business, and are much less likely to get ripped off.

Even if everything I've discussed didn't sink in the first time you read it, it is my hope that you will refer to this book time and time again as a guide to alert you to any red flags suggesting that someone might be trying to take advantage of you. Use it to ask questions of lawyers, record company personnel and anyone else in the business you come in contact with. If people ask you to sign a contract or give up rights that don't seem to line up with the suggested deal points or numbers in this book, don't just sign on the dotted line — call them on it.

Best of luck with your music career.

♪ ♪ ♪

I have compiled this book as an educational tool. Because of the constantly changing customs and laws related to this field, the information presented in this book should not be construed as legal advice, but merely educational information. For advice on any specific question, please contact an attorney.

APPENDIX I -- CONTRACTS

Most people don't know exactly what a contract is. That is why I have included this appendix.

What Is A Contract?

A contract, any contract, is simply a voluntary agreement between people to trade anything of value (for example — money, possessions, or your services). That's it. If you have an agreement, you have a contract. A contract can go by any number of different names. Here are just a few other names: deal, agreement, arrangement, and understanding. A contract doesn't have to be called a contract to be one.

If a friend of yours says, I'll sell you my guitar for $500, it becomes a contract once you say: "OK," or "deal", or "done" or anything else indicating that you accept your friend's offer to sell you his guitar. Like most contracts in the U.S. that can be performed in less than one year, it doesn't have to be in writing to be binding on both of you.[83]

Because a contract exists, if either you or your friend doesn't do what was agreed to, then the other can sue to enforce the contract.

---

[83] Some contracts do need to be in writing even if they can be performed in less than one year. For instance, transfers of copyright ownership (§204 of the Copyright Act); and in California, where I am an attorney, personal services contracts — such as publishing and record deals, to the extent that an injunction might be sought to stop you from recording for another company (Cal. Civil Code §3423). Also, certain real estate deals and wills need to be in writing (Cal. Civil Code §1624).

Reasons Contracts Are Put In Writing

There are two main reasons to put contracts in writing — apart from when required by law: First, the process of putting a contract in writing makes it less likely that there will be a misunderstanding about what was agreed to (i.e., someone saying, "but I never agreed to that").

Suppose you saw your friend playing his vintage Martin D-28 guitar in a coffee shop. Later that evening he offers to sell you his guitar for $500, and you accept. What if you thought you were buying your friend's exquisite Martin, but your friend thought he was selling you his Sears Craftsman? In that case, the two of you never agreed to anything, and no contract was formed. You didn't have what the law calls the *"meeting-of-the-minds."*

The other reason to put a contract in writing is that doing so makes it easier to prove in court the terms of the contract. If a written contract said your friend would sell you his Martin D-28, it would be hard for him to argue in front of a judge or jury that the agreement called for selling you something else.

There Is No Such Thing As A Standard Contract

There is no such thing as a standard written contract that cannot be changed. If someone tells you something is standard, my advice is to ignore the statement. Remember this when a publisher or record company executive hands you a contract and tells you that this is the standard company contract and can't be changed. Consider the executive's statement to be just a method of negotiation.

Use Riders Or Addendums

Sometimes it's easier in negotiation to add language at the end of someone else's contract rather than changing the contract form itself. Some people hate the thought of anyone messing with their form, yet don't seem to mind if someone adds to it. If handled the right way, the added language at the end wipes out what is said in the form contract. The addition is often called a *rider* or an *addendum* — but you can call it anything you like. In a rider, make sure to start by saying something like, "To the extent that the terms contained in this Rider are in conflict with the main text of the Contract, the terms of this Rider control and govern." By including this type of language, if the main text of the contract says one thing, and the rider says something that contradicts the main text, it's as if the main text of the contract said nothing at all.

If You Don't Understand It, Don't Sign It

When you enter into a contract, make sure you understand what you are signing. Use plain English and minimize legalese wherever you can. Legalese impresses lawyers and insecure muckety-mucks. The words "in the event that" is just a fancy way to say "if"; "the party of the first part" is a poor substitute for using a person's name. It made sense in your great grandparents' time, an era that had no computers, word processing or copy machines. It doesn't make sense now. Everyone who signs a contract ought to understand what he or she is signing. Understanding what you sign will keep future disputes to a minimum. Also, if there is a lawsuit somewhere down the road, a judge or jury will more likely understand the plain meaning of the agreement without the other side's lawyer being able to twist its meaning.

RECOMMENDED READING

Here are other outstanding sources of information from which you may benefit (apart from those I've already mentioned elsewhere in the book):

Confessions of a Record Producer, by Moses Avalon.

The Musicians Handbook, by Bobby Borg.

Music, Money, and Success, by Jeffrey and Todd Brabec.

This Business of Music, by M. William Krasilovsky, and Sidney Shemel.

All You Need To Know About The Music Business, by Donald S. Passman

New Songwriter's Guide to Music Publishing, by Randy Poe.

Music Law: How To Run Your Band's Business, by Richard Stim.

If you are thinking of putting out your own record, take a look at:

Start and Run Your Own Record Label, by Dayelle Deanna Schwartz.

Index

ABOUT THE AUTHOR

David Naggar is an attorney in the San Francisco Bay Area. He graduated Phi Beta Kappa from the University of California, Berkeley, where he received a Bachelor of Science degree in Business Administration. He received his Juris Doctor from the University of California, Berkeley Law (Boalt Hall) in 1981. Since graduating from law school, Mr. Naggar has, in addition to practicing law, interned in the Creative Department of the music publishing giant, Warner/Chappell Music. On the lighter side, Mr. Naggar fancies himself a semi-skilled musician, having played drums professionally for many years.

♪ ♪ ♪

I really want you to read and learn from this book — not just have it sit on a shelf. That is why I made it concise, rather than 400 pages of typically confusing lawyerese. I have made every effort to explain what you need to know in plain English.

Again, best of luck with your music career!